JUDICIAL REFORM AS POLITICAL INSURANCE

RECENT TITLES FROM THE HELEN KELLOGG INSTITUTE FOR
INTERNATIONAL STUDIES

Scott Mainwaring, *general editor*

The University of Notre Dame Press gratefully thanks the Helen Kellogg Institute for
International Studies for its support in the publication of titles in this series.

Caroline C. Beer
Electoral Competition and Institutional Change in Mexico (2003)

Yemile Mizrahi
From Martyrdom to Power: The Partido Acción Nacional in Mexico (2003)

Charles D. Kenney
Fujimori's Coup and the Breakdown of Democracy in Latin America (2004)

Alfred P. Montero and David J. Samuels, eds.
Decentralization and Democracy in Latin America (2004)

Katherine Hite and Paola Cesarini, eds.
Authoritarian Legacies and Democracy in Latin America and Southern Europe (2004)

Robert S. Pelton, C.S.C., ed.
Monsignor Romero: A Bishop for the Third Millennium (2004)

Guillermo O'Donnell, Jorge Vargas Cullell, and Osvaldo M. Iazzetta, eds.
The Quality of Democracy: Theory and Applications (2004)

Arie M. Kacowicz
The Impact of Norms in International Society: The Latin American Experience, 1881–2001 (2005)

Roberto DaMatta and Elena Soárez
Eagles, Donkeys, and Butterflies: An Anthropological Study of Brazil's "Animal Game" (2006)

Kenneth P. Serbin
Needs of the Heart: A Social and Cultural History of Brazil's Clergy and Seminaries (2006)

Christopher Welna and Gustavo Gallón, eds.
Peace, Democracy, and Human Rights in Colombia (2007)

Guillermo O'Donnell
Dissonances: Democratic Critiques of Democracy (2007)

Marifel Pérez-Stable, ed.
Looking Forward: Comparative Perspectives on Cuba's Transition (2007)

Robert R. Wilson, Peter M. Ward, Peter K. Spink, and Victoria E. Rodríguez
*Governance in the Americas: Decentralization, Democracy, and Subnational Government in
Brazil, Mexico, and the USA* (2008)

For a complete list of titles from the Helen Kellogg Institute for International Studies,
see http://www.undpress.nd.edu

Judicial Reform

as

Political Insurance

*Argentina, Peru, and Mexico
in the 1990s*

JODI S. FINKEL

University of Notre Dame Press

Notre Dame, Indiana

Library of Congress Cataloging-in-Publication Data

Finkel, Jodi S.
　　Judicial reform as political insurance : Argentina, Peru, and Mexico
in the 1990s / Jodi S. Finkel.
　　　　p.　　cm. — (From the Helen Kellogg Institute for International Studies)
　　Includes bibliographical references and index.
　　ISBN-13: 978-0-268-02887-9 (pbk. : alk. paper)
　　ISBN-10: 0-268-02887-7 (pbk. : alk. paper)
　　1. Justice, Administration of—Latin America.　　2. Political questions and
judicial power—Latin America.　　3. Latin America—Politics and government—
1980–　　4. Justice, Administration of—Argentina.　　5. Justice, Administration
of—Peru.　　6. Justice, Administration of—Mexico.　　I. Helen Kellogg Institute
for International Studies.　　II. Title.
　　KG495.F56　　2008
　　347.8—dc22

　　　　　　　　　　　　　　　　　　　　　　　　2008006892

 This book is printed on recycled paper.

Dedicated to my father

Dr. Max Finkel

in honor of his wisdom, generosity, and integrity

Contents

Acknowledgments

I thank the many people who inspired, assisted, and supported me while I was working on this project. The first are my parents, Betty and Max, two people on whom I could always count. A big thank-you also goes to my brother, David, for believing in the value of my research, for editing my entire dissertation, and for numerous "David J. Finkel Travel Awards for Young Scholars" in support of my adventures on the research trail. I also say *muchísimas gracias* to Julie Manevitz and Robin McLaughlin for all their encouragement.

I particularly thank my advisers at UCLA, Barbara Geddes and Mike Thies, as well as my dear friend Julie Taylor, for helping me to conceptualize my work.

I owe thanks to many people and institutions in Argentina, Peru, and Mexico. In Argentina, these include Alberto Dalla Vía, Adrián Ventura, Carlos Vayafín, and Tulio Ortíz; the University of Buenos Aires Law School for hosting me while I conducted research; and Silvina Natalicchio and Diana Kapiszweski for archival research at *La Nación* headquarters. I thank Victor Cubas, Jose Ugaz, Carlos Montoya Anguerry, David Lovatón Palacios, and Esperanza Chavez (my "Peruvian grandmother") in Peru, as well as the Institute for Legal Defense and La Católica Law School in Lima, both of which hosted me as a visiting scholar. I also thank Lucho Quequezana for incidentally helping me fall in love with Andean music in the course of my research. I particularly thank John Moody, a rich source for my general knowledge of Mexico, Pamela Starr, and José Ramón Cossío-Díaz, source for much of my specific knowledge of the Mexican judicial system. I also thank the Center for Economic Information and Teaching (CIDE) in Mexico City for hosting me for two summers as a visiting researcher.

My research and writing time was funded by many sources, including UCLA's Chancellor's Dissertation Fellowship, a Charles F. Scott Fellowship, an International Fieldwork Fellowship from UCLA's International Studies and Opportunities Program, a Ford Foundation Travel Grant, and a Summer Research Grant from UCLA's Latin American Center. I am grateful for all of them.

Introduction

Latin America and Judicial Reform:
Why Would Politicians Enact Institutional Reforms
That Appear to Limit Their Own Political Power?

Judicial reform, defined here as institutional changes claiming to increase the independence and authority of the judicial branch, swept Latin America in the 1990s. Argentina, Peru, and Mexico, for example, each engaged in constitutional revisions that appeared to empower their judiciaries. Following their respective judicial reforms, high courts in each country were asked to decide the constitutionality of a ruling party's attempt to manipulate political rules. In Argentina, the Supreme Court refused to rule against the president; in Peru, the Constitutional Court justices who did so were fired and their decision ignored. The Mexican Supreme Court, on the other hand, ruled against that country's long-standing dominant party, and its decision was accepted and enforced. Politicians in each of these countries had introduced what appeared to be very similar judicial reforms—yet these three court cases present extreme variations in judicial power. Why do some instances of judicial reform succeed at establishing a judiciary able to constrain elected leaders while others fail to do so? Even more striking, why would politicians who previously enjoyed decision-making powers unfettered by judicial constraints willfully engage in reforms that place limits on their own political power?

This book attempts to answer this question by analyzing the judicial reform experiences of three Latin American countries: Argentina, Peru, and Mexico. As was typical throughout the region, these countries' judicial reforms began with constitutional revisions consisting of a package of institutional changes dramatically altering judicial structures. However, passage of constitutional reforms is but the first step in the process of meaningful judicial reform. In Latin America, judicial reform is a two-stage process of *initiation* (the passage of constitutional revisions) followed by *implementation* (the enactment of congressional legislation). The crucial point is that while passage of constitutional reforms may signal an intent to increase judicial autonomy, the real outcome of judicial reform is determined by the details and vigor of the implementing legislation. In our three cases, while Mexico's judicial reform was meaningfully implemented, Argentina's and Peru's were not. This book is an attempt to explain variations in the implementation of Latin America's judicial reforms and, thus, variations in the power of each country's postreform judiciary.

Historically, the judiciaries of Latin America have been impotent and unable to prevent even the most blatant constitutional violations by the prevailing political elite.[1] Repeatedly trampled on and ignored by politicians, the courts of Latin America were also routinely neglected by scholars. However, as elected governments replaced authoritarian regimes across the globe at the end of the twentieth century, interest in the judiciary in the developing world underwent a dramatic reversal. Latin American courts, after decades of academic neglect, have today become a major concern of research in the region.[2] Democratic theorists, viewing institutional reform as key to the consolidation of "third-wave" democracies, have focused on the development of judicial counterweights capable of imposing limits on elected leaders and upholding the rule of law (Schedler, Diamond, and Plattner 1999; Larkins 1996; Stotzky 1993). Multilateral development agencies have published numerous works stressing the need to foster a legal environment conducive to the development of a market economy (Jarquín and Carrillo 1998; Rowat, Malik, and Dakolias 1995). Additional scholarly work has examined the international promotion of other aspects of judicial reform, such as access to justice and judicial efficiency in Latin America (United States Agency for International Development 2002; Domingo and Sieder 2001).

There are now also a number of academic studies describing a particular country's judiciary (Mexico: Domingo 2000 and Finkel 2003; Peru: Hammergren 1998a; El Salvador: Popkin 2000; Chile: Hilbink 2003). Research on Argentina has been especially abundant. Bill-Chavez examines two Argentine provinces and argues that divided government is key for the development of judicial autonomy (2003). Helmke's analysis of the Argentine Supreme Court during the years 1976–95 demonstrates that antigovernment rulings cluster at the end of both weak democratic and weak nondemocratic governments alike (2002). Iaryczower, Spiller, and Tomassi, examining Argentina between 1935 and 1998, show that the probability of a justice voting against the government increases the less aligned the justice is with the president but decreases the stronger the president's control over the legislature (2002). Using the case of Mexico, Staton argues that supreme courts selectively issue press releases to publicize specific decisions as a strategy to bolster judiciary authority (2006). As for more inclusive studies, Prillaman gives an overview of the judiciary in several Latin American countries by discussing inputs and outputs to measure reform (2000). Central American judiciaries, and the challenges they present for that region's transitioning governments, have also been detailed in recent works (Dodson and Jackson 2001; Siedler 1996).

We are deepening our knowledge of the Latin American judiciary, but the question of when politicians take actions to promote the development of a more powerful judicial branch remains understudied. I argue that in order to understand the outcomes of judicial reform, as well as to predict where reforms are likely to empower courts, it is necessary to examine the political incentives faced by politicians at the implementation phase. If ruling parties believe that they are unlikely to maintain political power, then they have a strong rationale for proceeding with judicial empowerment. Implementation of judicial reform in such a situation may serve the ruling party as an "insurance policy" in which a stronger judicial branch reduces the risks the ruling party faces should it become the opposition. This book suggests that the likelihood of meaningful implementation, the crucial determinant of judicial reform, increases as the ruling party's probability of re-election declines. By separating the constitutional adoption of judicial advancement from its legislative enactment, this book contributes to a better understanding of the conditions under which proclaimed judicial independence is converted into real judicial oversight.

This introductory chapter proceeds in five sections. The first section provides an overview of the judicial concepts necessary to evaluate Latin America's recent reforms. The second describes the region's traditional judiciary and details the general package of reforms pursued in the 1990s. The third section summarizes two alternative explanations for the region's reforms as well as my "insurance policy" theory, and briefly addresses the ability of these three arguments to explain differences in the power of Latin America's postreform judiciaries. The fourth section presents the case selection and research method, and the last gives an overview of the book.

The Judiciary in a Democratic Government: The Rule of Law, Checks and Balances, and Judicial Power

The rule of law, or the absolute supremacy of law over arbitrary power, underpins democratic government.[3] In a democracy based on the rule of law, all subjects are treated equally and no individual (even one enjoying political power) is above the law. The courts, as the primary guardian of the rule of law, are responsible for safeguarding individual liberties against unconstitutional encroachment in a democratic political system. Thus, the duty of the judiciary is to guarantee that law, and not raw power, is the foundation of government. Additionally, judiciaries provide for conflict resolution, social control, and supplementary detailing of the law (Shapiro 1981, chap. 1; Hammergren 2002a).

In presidential democracies, where government structure is based on the separation-of-powers principle, a central mandate of the judiciary is to ensure that legislative and executive authority remain within their constitutional limits. In a system of checks and balances, it is the obligation of the judicial apparatus to exert "constitutional control": to interpret the constitution, to place limits on the other branches, and to determine when those limits have been violated. In all presidential systems, the judiciary ostensibly serves the same purpose, yet in practice the judicial branch only fulfills its role where it wields real power.

Judicial independence has been widely discussed in scholarly literature (Landes and Posner 1975; Iaryczower, Spiller, and Tomassi 2002; Fiss

1993; Larkins 1996).[4] Definitions of judicial independence range from the minimal to the expansive, extending from an exclusive focus on the judiciary's structural features to a broader concern with the behavior of courts vis-à-vis other government institutions. Peter Russell, seeking to build a general theory of judicial independence, uses the term in two distinct ways: (1) as a relationship between judges and judicial institutions with respect to other individuals, groups, and interests in society; and (2) as demonstrated behavior by judges to rule independently of those who enjoy power (Russell 2001). Each of these two definitions has been used by scholars examining Latin America. Helmke uses the latter for her work on Argentina (2002), while Dodson and Jackson use the former for their research on Central America (2001). This book, in seeking to determine under what conditions the courts are enabled to act "as a countervailing force within the larger governmental structure" (Fiss 1993, 56), encompasses both of Russell's definitions of judicial independence.

However, for the purpose of this study, I prefer to use the term *judicial power*, rather than *judicial independence*, to best capture the idea of a court whose actions demonstrate that it enjoys independence as well as authority. Thus, *judicial independence* is used here in a narrow sense to signify that judges make decisions according to expressed rules and free from external manipulation. It requires that judges be named in an impartial manner and that they be protected from political retribution while on the bench. Formal arrangements to operationalize independence include tenure (security in office), selection procedures (appointment and career advancement), and salary (financial compensation may not be diminished while in office). In this more restricted sense of judicial independence, however, independence in itself does not ensure the existence of a judiciary capable of fulfilling its role as an effective check on the use of political power in a presidential democracy. For a court to enjoy real power, it must also possess authority.

Authority, or the rightful exercise of power with the claim to be obeyed, refers to the legitimacy of a government branch. Judicial authority requires that court rulings be accepted and complied with by affected parties, members of society, and power holders in the larger political structure. Furthermore, authority requires that courts possess broad jurisdiction: a wide range of subject matter upon which the courts may rule. If a court was able to make impartial decisions yet by law was permitted to make decisions only on a severely circumscribed set of issues, then judicial authority would be meaningless in practice. Thus, for a court to have the potential to wield real power, its jurisdiction must envelop salient social, political, and economic questions. In sum, the exercise of judicial power refers to the promulgation of decisions by impartial judges, covering a wide range of issues and based on written laws, which are obeyed by societal interests as well as by those who wield political authority.

The Traditional Judiciary in Latin America
and the Reforms of the 1990s

The Weakest Branch

Upon achieving independence in the early nineteenth century, Latin American countries established separation-of-powers presidential democracies and granted formal independence to their courts. Although Latin America's founding documents included a tripartite institutional structure, judiciaries in the region never achieved the political power formally ascribed to them in their national constitutions. Indeed, the judiciary was neither separate nor equal, nor was it expected to be (Wiarda and Kline 1985). However, that is not to say that the courts wielded no power. Hammergren refers to Latin American judiciaries as enjoying "bounded independence"—in other words, exercising some autonomy in areas that did not threaten government interests (Hammergren 1998b). Still, from the perspective of democratic checks and balances, political domination left the courts generally unable to constrain either elected officials or de facto governments.

The subordination of the Latin American judiciary to the prevailing political powers is a result of a combination of factors, including executive dominance, instability of judicial posts, civil law and a formalistic legal culture, and lack of popular support for the judiciary (Verner 1984; Hammergren 2002a). First, Latin American presidents have wielded overwhelming political power, with executives refusing to respect formal constitutional limits or submit to counterbalancing by the other branches

(Wiarda and Kline 1985; Domingo 1999). Determined to inhibit court capacity to check executive authority, presidents have repeatedly manipulated judicial institutions. In particular, executives have used control over the selection and promotion of judges to debilitate judicial will to challenge political leadership (Frühling 1993). Second, Latin America's judicial branch has also suffered from extreme institutional instability. Repeated cycling of governments in the twentieth century resulted in purges and packings that frequently altered judicial postings (Domingo 1999; Prillaman 2000). In addition, the justices themselves, who often saw the court as a temporary stepping-stone to a more lucrative political office rather than as an end in itself, opted to serve short tenures and thus contributed to the high rate of turnover on the bench. Hand-picked and often temporary, the region's judiciaries were unable to develop the institutional autonomy from which to build their own base of power.

Third, Latin America's legal system, rooted in civil law, has traditionally denied the courts the right to vigorously engage in constitutional control. Historically, judges in civil law systems, in contrast to those of common law, do not have the power of *stare decisis* (the power and obligation of courts to base decisions on prior decisions) or the power of judicial review (the authority to declare a law null and void should it be found unconstitutional).[5] Although a civil law judge may declare a law unconstitutional as applied in a particular case, the law itself is not invalidated and remains in effect for the rest of the population. Thus, Latin American judges have not been empowered to "strike a law from the books."[6] (It should be noted that while traditional civil law rejected both *stare decisis* and judicial review, increasingly modern civil legal systems are beginning to accept these two common law principles, and since World War II many countries of Continental Europe have established special constitutional courts that are exclusively empowered to determine the constitutionality of legislation.)[7]

Additionally, civil law's more restrictive role for judges is exacerbated by Latin America's rigid legal culture, which applies the *letter*, rather than the *spirit*, of the law. Supreme court justices have adopted a legal philosophy that limits their powers of constitutional control to reviewing compliance with formal requirements instead of examining the constitutional principles at stake (Saez Garcia 1998). Hilbink, in her work on the Chilean judiciary, claims that a judicial ideology that equated judicial professionalism with apoliticism rendered judges unequipped to assert authority and check abuses of power (1999). Judges in Latin America's conservative legal culture, rather than viewing their role as one of determining whether laws are just, have viewed their role as one of making sure that laws are properly enforced.

Fourth, public perception of the courts as inefficient and corrupt has contributed to the weak position of the judicial branch in the region (Dakolias 1996; Buscaglia, Dakolias, and Ratliff 1995). According to surveys conducted in the first half of the 1990s in Argentina, Bolivia, Peru, and Venezuela, more than 80 percent of the population prefers to avoid the formal justice system (Ciurlizza 1999, 5). Public dissatisfaction with the justice system is notorious (Pásara 1998), and the judiciary suffers from an absence of popular support (Méndez 1999) and low credibility. A judiciary that is perceived as inept and dishonest lacks the authority to sanction abuses of authority, creating leeway for presidents and other political figures to engage in such abuses.

Finally, augmenting the conventional explanations for the traditional weakness of the judicial branch in Latin America, we must add that judges' concerns for self-preservation reduce their will to confront powerful politicians. Hence, even in the cases where Latin American supreme courts have formally possessed the power of judicial review, judges have been hesitant to exert their authority, as attempting to impose limits could result in dismissal from the bench (at best) and/or more severe forms of political retribution (Wiarda and Kline 1985; Verner 1984).[8] In consequence, Latin American judiciaries have broadly defined their range of proscribed issues and frequently engaged in voluntary self-censorship.

Thus, the historical development of Latin America's courts resulted in judiciaries that relinquished any claim to resolve political conflicts or constrain the executive branch. This remained true even though the region's judiciaries were subjected to multiple constitutional reforms throughout the twentieth century. While past reforms claimed to strengthen Latin America's courts, each successively failed to alter the pattern of judicial impotence that had long beset the region. Once again in the 1990s, Latin America embarked on a new round of judicial reform that, at least in national constitutions, redefined the independence and authority of each country's judicial branch.

The Judicial Reforms of the 1990s

Latin America's recent wave of judicial reform, enacted with the stated intent of increasing judicial power, dramatically restructured national judiciaries throughout the region.[9] In general, these constitutional reform packages centered on changes affecting the supreme court (and the constitutional court where it existed), the selection of judges, and the administration of the judicial branch. With respect to high court changes, judicial reforms altered the composition of these courts' membership (either by a total replacement of justices or by adding new members to the court), the selection process of justices, the ability of the executive and legislature to change the rules that govern the court, and the extent of judicial review powers. As for the latter, the countries of Latin America have experimented with different mechanisms to establish judicial review, including creating separate constitutional tribunals as well as explicitly granting judicial review powers to existing supreme courts.[10]

As for changes to lower-level judicial selection and administration, national judicial councils were established throughout the region.[11] Even though Latin America's judicial councils vary with respect to their specific functions, at a minimum most are charged with (1) the selection, discipline, and removal of judges below the supreme court level, and (2) professionalization of the judicial career track.[12] Council membership also varies across countries, but council composition may include judicial representatives, members of the executive and legislative branches, and legal professionals and academics.[13] Taken together, these supreme court and lower-level institutional changes appear to decrease executive influence while increasing the quality of judicial rulings and the efficiency of the judicial branch.

In addition to this "recipe" of institutional changes, Latin America's recent judicial reforms were also alike in that they encompassed two distinct phases. The first, initiation, can be viewed as a "proclamation period" in which coming judicial changes are formally announced via the rewriting of the national constitution. The second, implementation, entails the passage of congressional legislation that translates abstract constitutional concepts into concrete structures. Thus, although the promulgation of constitutional changes may declare profound institutional changes and elegant new principles, these remain in limbo until the passage of the implementing legislation.

Despite professed goals of empowering the judiciary, for the greater part of the twentieth century Latin American judicial reforms did little to reduce the dominance of presidents over the courts. The 1990s reforms, at least in Argentina, Peru, and Mexico, were similar in form to one another and appeared to grant greater powers to the courts. But the implementation of these reforms—and therefore the resulting impact on the balance of power—varied considerably. To understand why these differences came to be, the next section briefly presents three potential arguments, one societal, one economic, and one political, to explain the region's judicial reforms during the last decade of the twentieth century.

Possible Explanations for the Range of Outcomes of Judicial Reform

One potential explanation for the recent wave of judicial reform in Latin America is that such reform was provided in response to demands of societal groups that pressed for a more effective judicial branch. However, to understand reforms desired by domestic civil organizations, it is important to distinguish between the macro-level structural reforms mentioned above (for example, changes to supreme courts and creation of judicial councils) and other types of "justice" reforms that may be contained under the rubric of judicial reform. This latter category broadly includes "improving access to justice and legal aid programmes, strengthening alternative dispute resolution and mediation facilities, enhancing professional development and training, increasing the awareness of legal and judicial reform issues, improving technical and management assistance, and conducting research on the issues and practices in the field" (Dakolias 2001, 85). Justice reforms may also include such topics as revising the penal code, police reform, and human rights trials.

While the activities of the nongovernmental organizations (NGOs) have focused on justice reforms (Dakolias 2001), they have not played a major role in the process of constitutional revisions to restructure judicial institutions in either Mexico (Finkel 2005) or South America (Pásara

2003). In my in-country interviews (conducted across a wide range of sources, including political, legal, business, and human rights representatives), I found little emphasis on the role of civil society in the structural reforms pursued in Argentina, Peru, or Mexico. For example, interviewees were asked open-ended questions such as: Who pushed for judicial reform? How did it get on the agenda? But their responses did not highlight NGO activity as a prominent factor behind the constitutional reforms to the judiciary in any of the three countries. Latin American legal expert Luis Pásara, in his examination of judicial reforms in Argentina, Chile, Colombia, and Peru, argues that "civil society did not have a significant presence in the reforms produced" (2003, 15).[14]

Indeed, this lack of civil society involvement in the institutional reforms of the 1990s was true even for those groups most likely to be concerned with such reform, for example, human rights organizations and legal associations. As for Latin American human rights NGOs, it is true that these groups actively pressed for strengthening habeas corpus protections, for bringing former leaders to trial for human rights violations, and for delineating appropriate spheres of jurisdiction between civil and military tribunals. In particular, these goals were vigorously pursued where elected governments had recently replaced brutal military regimes. Yet, as affirmed by prominent members of the human rights community in all three countries under study here, domestic human rights concerns were not the impetus for undertaking major institutional reforms of the judiciary in either Argentina, Peru, or Mexico (Zamorano 1999; Basombrio 1997a; Harel 1998).[15]

As for other civil organizations that would be most interested in judicial reform, such as bar associations, judges' groups, and law schools, their participation in the constitutional reforms redefining the judiciary was also quite limited. At the request of the executive branch, individual members of these organizations drafted judicial proposals for which they were financially compensated, but as groups they had not been pressing for constitutional reforms. In fact, these organizations frequently opposed the reforms precisely because they had not been consulted about them (Cossío-Diaz 1998b) and because they perceived that the reforms undermined their interests. For example, members of supreme courts opposed the reforms because new judicial councils usurped their traditional powers and because the reforms often resulted in their expulsion from the bench. In addition, legal associations resisted many aspects of judicial reform because they implied new burdens as well as a loss of control over financial perks (Moody 2000; Pásara 2003). Rigorous examinations for judicial promotion make advancement more difficult, and moving from lengthy written procedures to speedier oral ones means that lawyers have to learn to think on their feet. Additionally, decreasing the number of required procedural filings reduces the processing fees received by lawyers as well as the opportunities for accepting bribes to move paperwork forward.

In sum, while domestic interest groups pressed for a range of justice reforms, and in some cases opposed specific judicial reforms, civil society did not place constitutional revisions of judicial institutions on the political agenda, and the activities of civilian actors cannot explain the variation in judicial outcomes that occurred throughout the region.

A second popular argument to explain the Latin American experience with judicial reform is based on the premise that these measures were undertaken in order to ensure successful economic reforms. Since the 1980s, the governments of Latin America have embarked on dramatic economic restructuring, replacing their state-led economic models with more market-based policies. The conventional wisdom holds that the consolidation of Latin America's new private-sector-led economies requires the existence of independent judiciaries—judiciaries capable of upholding property rights and enforcing business contracts—to facilitate economic transactions and foster private investment. Indeed, government officials throughout Latin America have noted this connection explicitly. However, the fact that judicial reform has produced different results in these countries, despite similar economic motivations across borders, means that an economic argument alone cannot explain the resulting variation in institutional power in postreform judiciaries.

While today it is widely accepted that judicial reform is good for a country's economy and that such reform will therefore benefit a country, it must be remembered that reforms are not undertaken by "countries" but by politicians. Economic explanations fail because they only consider the "best interests of countries" rather than investigating the motivations of politicians. If countries were the agents for judicial reform, then all of the judicial reforms would have been successfully implemented. Instead, we have variations in the outcomes of judicial reform precisely because politicians—although they would benefit from a healthy economy—must weigh the economic benefits from judicial reform against its political costs. These costs, the possibility of judicial interference with a ruling party's ability to achieve preferred policies, are potentially severe. However, these costs are not constant over both periods of reform; rather, they only take effect following meaningful implementation.

During the initiation period, when constitutional changes are first enacted, the costs of reform are minimized as they are neither immediate nor certain. Costs are incurred only once the implementing legislation (which specifies exactly how to complete these constitutional reforms) is enacted by a simple majority vote in congress. Hence, at implementation, presidents who enjoy a congressional majority can undermine increases in judicial power that were agreed on at initiation. Rather than yielding to an empowered judiciary at implementation, ruling parties may subvert the reform process at this second stage.

While these insights help explain why impressive constitutional changes stumble after initiation, they still cannot explain why some judicial reforms are meaningfully implemented. After considering the political costs of such reform, and the ability of politicians to stymie implementation, we must ask, why would any politician seek meaningful implementation? I hold that chances of retaining political power determine whether politicians will proceed with or will dilute promised judicial reforms during the implementation phase.

When a ruling party is confident about its continued control over political power, it should be hesitant to enact legislation that will curtail its room to maneuver and therefore has little incentive to follow through with promised judicial empowerment at implementation. On the other hand, when a ruling party's chances of continuing to control office are low, the ruling party has the incentive to follow through with judicial advancements. In such a situation, a stronger judicial branch decreases the risks the ruling party faces should it become the opposition. An independent judiciary may check the capacity of incoming politicians to harm the interests of the outgoing ruling party. For example, an independent judiciary can prevent the incoming party from changing the rules of the game in ways that would hinder the outgoing party from returning to office in the future. It can also prevent the incoming party from altering policies established by the outgoing party. Thus, in an uncertain political environment, a weakening ruling party may undertake judicial reform as an "insurance policy." By empowering the judiciary, the current ruling party hedges against likely downturns in its own political position. This book suggests that the implementation of judicial reform depends on the ruling party's perception of its probability of retaining political control. As chances of maintaining political power decline, the likelihood of meaningful implementation of judicial reform increases. This book attempts to test this argument about judicial reform in Argentina, Peru, and Mexico.

Case Selection and Research Method

While many Latin American countries experienced judicial reform during the 1990s, I opted to focus on three cases: Argentina, Mexico, and Peru. Each of these countries' reforms is representative of the general pattern of judicial reform that occurred in the larger countries of the region. This is true with respect to both the timing of reform and the overall package of constitutional changes affecting the judiciary. Furthermore, Argentina, Mexico, and Peru, like most of Latin America in the 1990s, were engaged in dramatic economic restructuring. Thus, these three cases allow me to hold constant economic reform as a cause of demand for judicial reform within each country while varying political institutions and actors—and it is the effect of these factors on judicial reform that is of interest here.

Finally, these three countries were chosen in order to have variation on the outcome of judicial reform: Mexico's reforms went the furthest in granting real power to the judiciary; Argentina's reforms were delayed five years before being implemented; and Peru's reforms were eviscerated by executive interference shortly after they were undertaken. All three countries initiated judicial reform, but there was substantial variation in how these reforms were implemented, resulting in dramatic variation in the power of their postreform courts. It is this variation that this book seeks to explain.

I conducted field research in all three countries during the period 1996–2000. The goal of my research abroad was to investigate four aspects of reform: (1) how judicial reform came to be on the political agenda; (2) the bargains that led to the initial package of constitutional changes; (3) the details of the implementing legislation; and (4) the real effect of the reforms on the independence and authority of the judicial branch.

First, I wanted to determine how judicial reform came to be a political priority. Was it a response to pressures from domestic interests (for example, human rights groups or the business community) or from multilateral financial institutions (such as the World Bank and the International Monetary Fund)? Or was judicial reform a result of bargaining among the political elite? To answer these questions, I interviewed representatives from a wide range of societal groups, multilateral organizations, and political parties. From these interviews I concluded that the decision to introduce constitutional reforms, and the subsequent decision whether to follow through with legislation to empower the judiciary, reflected the will of domestic politicians seeking to further their unique political interests.

Second, I analyzed the bargains over judicial restructuring that were negotiated during the constitutional sessions. I began by identifying each party's original judicial proposal in order to determine its initial preferred outcome. I then followed the evolution of judicial changes at the constitutional convention, relying both on the published constitutional debates and on personal interviews with individuals who served on the constitutional conventions' judicial committees. I also interviewed legal experts who were asked by political parties to draft judicial reform proposals for use at the conventions. This book shows that presidents, at least at initiation, were willing to agree to institutional increases in judicial power. Additionally, in order to obtain the support of opposition forces whose approval was necessary for passage of the new constitution, presidents were often forced to write in further increases in judicial power. Hence, the resulting constitutional changes empowering the judicial branch in all three countries.

Third, I tracked each country's implementing legislation following the initiation of its constitutional reforms (1993 or 1994) until 2000. In each case I discuss the debates surrounding this legislation, the legislation itself, and the political context at the time. It is this legislation, both in its details and timing, that is crucial in determining the real outcome (the degree of political power enjoyed by the restructured judiciary) of judicial reform.

Fourth, to develop a true understanding of the effect of reform on the judicial branch, it is not sufficient just to follow the paper trail in Latin America. Latin America's political reality is often quite distinct from what is written in its constitutions; hence, the only way to understand the power of a particular Latin American political institution is to conduct in-country research. Thus, my evaluation of the power of postreform courts also includes a broad range of interviews. I spoke with judges at all levels of the judicial apparatus as well as representatives of the national judicial councils and departments of justice. Additionally, I interviewed politicians from a range of political parties, constitutional experts, legal scholars, other academics, and representatives from domestic groups and international organizations. Finally, I tracked court cases, including both cases that the courts have ruled upon and those that the courts have refused to consider, on controversial issues and key political matters. By discussing the reform process with those involved and affected and by monitoring the behavior of postreform judiciaries, I was able to develop a nuanced understanding of each country's judicial reform.

An Overview of the Book

The book is divided into five chapters. Chapter 1 presents two potential arguments to explain Latin America's judicial reforms, one derived from economic concerns and the other from political interests. First, it provides an overview of the literature on law and economic performance in a market economy and discusses the role of international financial institutions (IFIs) in the process of judicial reform. The chapter next demonstrates the limitations of economics-based hypotheses and argues that the transition to a market economy and IFI pressures are insufficient to explain the implementation of a particular country's judicial reform. The chapter then provides a theory of institutional reform that relies on the incentives of political actors and applies this argument to judicial reform's two stages. Finally, it identifies the probability of retaining political power as the crucial variable for determining a ruling party's willingness to implement meaningful judicial reform.

Chapters 2, 3, and 4 test my argument with in-depth analyses of the judicial reform experiences in Argentina, Peru, and Mexico, respectively. In Argentina (chapter 2), judicial reform was a negotiated deal between the Peronist and Radical parties, included as part of that country's 1994 constitutional reform. In exchange for the right to re-election, Argentina's then-president Carlos Menem, of the Peronist Party, agreed to Radical Party demands for reappointing the Supreme Court (which he had packed four years earlier) as well as the creation of an independent national judicial council to appoint lower-level judges. However, after Menem's successful re-election bid in 1995, the president failed to recompose the Supreme Court and used his party's control of Congress to delay the creation of the council. It was not until five years later, at a time when it appeared that the Peronist Party would lose the presidency in that year's national election, that the National Judicial Council was finally established and the president effectively relinquished control over the judicial branch.

Chapter 3 presents the Peruvian case study. In Peru, as in Argentina, judicial changes empowering the courts were part of a larger rewriting of the country's constitution. Peru's 1993 constitutional convention was established following the April 1992 "self-coup" carried out by then-president Alberto Fujimori. In exchange for the right to seek a second term, the president agreed to the creation of a powerful National Judicial Council as well as the continued existence of the Constitutional Court (alongside the traditional Supreme Court). However, upon his 1995 re-election, Fujimori used his congressional majority to enact legislation systematically eviscerating all judicial autonomy and power. The Peruvian judiciary was placed under an executive committee in 1996, and shortly thereafter, as a result of executive actions, both the Judicial Council and the Constitutional Court ceased to function. Not until Fujimori announced that he would be stepping down, following a corruption scandal in September 2000, did Congress enact implementing legislation to remove the judiciary from executive control and to establish the judicial institutions specified in Peru's 1993 constitution.

Chapter 4 details the recent Mexican judicial reform experience carried out by Mexico's long-dominant ruling party, the Institutional

Revolutionary Party (PRI). In 1994, after seven decades of judicial subordination, Mexico's PRI president introduced a package of constitutional reforms that increased the independence and authority of the judicial branch. The reforms created the Federal Judicial Council to select judges and also granted the Mexican Supreme Court judicial review powers that the court had never previously enjoyed. The Congress, controlled by the ruling party, fully implemented the reforms just five months after initiation. Four years later Mexico's restructured Supreme Court unanimously ruled against the PRI on a key electoral law, clearly demonstrating that the country's 1994 judicial reforms had fundamentally altered Mexico's traditional balance of power.[16] At initiation, PRI politicians were increasingly unable to control political outcomes at the state and local level and were unsure whether they would maintain their dominance of the national government in the future. The ruling party had the incentive not only to introduce judicial reform, but also to follow through with its meaningful implementation.

Chapter 5 concludes by summarizing my research and drawing conclusions from my three case studies for attaining meaningful judicial reform in other countries in the developing world. First, while political leaders in Latin America have repeatedly recognized that judicial reform is a necessary complement to consolidate their new economic policies, economic concerns have proved expendable when they conflict with the political interests of those in power. For this reason, similar economic motivations cannot account for the significant variation in the de facto power of these countries' reformed judiciaries. Second, constitutional increases in judicial independence and power may later be undermined or postponed by implementing legislation that often remains in the hands of the ruling party. Thus, the benchmark for evaluating a country's progress on judicial reform should be its implementation, not its initiation.

Finally, empowering the courts requires politicians to cede political power and to accept new institutional constraints on the exercise of their authority. Thus, for political leaders to follow through with the enactment of judiciary-strengthening reforms, they must perceive political gains that offset the potential costs. In all three countries, only once the ruling parties believed that they were unlikely to maintain their position of political dominance did they seek full implementation of judicial advancements promised in the revised constitution. This book suggests that reforms granting the judiciary increased independence and authority are more likely to occur when the ruling party fears loss of office: as the probability of retaining control over political office decreases, the likelihood of meaningful implementation of judicial reform increases.

Institutional reforms ensuring judicial power are crucial for the achievement of full democracy in Latin America. By explaining variations in outcomes of judicial power in Argentina, Peru, and Mexico, this book seeks to determine the circumstances in which judicial reform leads to the development of a judiciary capable of placing constraints on those who wield political power. The significance of judicial reform is not limited just to countries in Latin America; rather, it extends to all developing countries attempting to consolidate new democracies as they enter the twenty-first century.

Chapter One

Explaining Latin America's Recent Judicial Reforms

This chapter presents two potential explanations for understanding the judicial reforms that swept Latin America in the 1990s. The first section outlines an argument based on the transition to a market economy and the pressures of international financial institutions (IFIs). First it provides an overview of the literature on institutions and economic performance, then it discusses the developing world's economic transition and the IFIs' role in judicial reform. The section concludes by demonstrating the severe limitations of this economics-based approach. In particular, this understanding cannot account for the wide variation in outcomes of the region's judicial reforms.

The second section begins by laying out a general theory of institutional reform and develops an argument that relies on the incentives of political actors. It then details the two phases of judicial reform—the necessary building blocks for understanding the region's recent reform experience—initiation and implementation. Next, the institutional argument is applied to both stages of the Latin American judicial reform process. It shows why initiation is readily achieved, as well as why the second stage has proved so much more difficult to attain: ruling politicians can easily be induced to engage in initiation; however, until they fear loss of office, they are disinclined to follow through with meaningful implementation. Because this approach can account for differences in implementation, the crucial determinant of postreform judicial power, it can better explain variations in the outcomes of Latin American judicial reforms and better predict when judicial empowerment is most likely to occur.

Economic Arguments to Explain Judicial Reform

Legal Institutions and Economic Performance in a Market Economy

Legal institutions and their reform have emerged as primary concerns in debates addressing the achievement of sustainable economic growth in the developing world.[1] In particular, the importance of legal structures and judicial systems to economic development has been brought to the forefront by the New Institutional Economics (NIE), an area of research that provides strong support for the claim that institutions—specifically property rights institutions—affect economic performance.[2] While research in NIE is broad,[3] its main concerns have been on institutions that reduce uncertainty and allow for credible commitments: both institutions that bind state power[4] and institutions that uphold contracts between private individuals (Messick 1999; Workshop on Law and Economic Development 2005). Modern capitalist economies—which rely on private investment as the engine of growth—require institutions that protect property rights and their transfer (the subject of contract law).[5] Specifically, protection of property rights encourages entrepreneurs to take advantage of investment opportunities and to upgrade productive capacity; contract law provides the necessary insurance to allow market transactions in goods, services, and capital. Where both the former and the latter are respected, resources are allocated to their most valuable use and long-term investment is encouraged, thereby contributing to better economic performance (Posner 1986; De Soto 1986; North 1990). Indeed, for NIE scholars, institutions are the crucial factor for explaining variations in economic growth across countries (North 1990; Libecap 1997; Coase 1998; Williamson 2000; Rodrik, Subramanian, and Trebbi 2002).

NIE's concern with property rights institutions has been extremely influential in policy prescriptions for the developing world in the last fifteen years. As countries replaced their state-led economic models with ones based on private investment, attention focused on providing the correct "institutional environment" and in particular on establishing an effective legal system as part of this proper institutional structure. Such a legal system, in turn, is itself built on twin pillars: an autonomous judiciary and a sound legal environment. A competent, independent judiciary provides the safeguards necessary to inspire investor confidence, as investors perceive that the merits of the case, rather than political pressures, personal relationships, or bribes, will determine judicial decision making. Additionally, while private investment is facilitated by efficient legal administration, it is deterred by cumbersome bureaucratic procedures and delays in judicial decisions. In order for court cases to be meaningful for entrepreneurs and investors, they must be resolved in a timely fashion. Furthermore, high-performing economies are characterized by a consistent body of law capable of addressing technology changes and by the existence of alternative mechanisms for dispute resolution, such as arbitration and mediation. Investors (obviously in addition to the lure of a positive rate of return) will invest only where they believe that they possess guarantees to enable them to obtain a return on their investments. "Indeed, serious investors look for a legal system where property rights, contractual agreements, and other lawful activities are safeguarded and respected, free from arbitrary governmental action and from pressure from special interest groups or powerful individuals" (Shihata 1995, 220).

Today, security of economic rights remains a critical distinction between rich and poor countries (North 1990; Shirley 2003). Developed countries enjoy legal systems that provide a secure and predictable business environment, reduce the costs of exchange, and foster the construction of an attractive investment climate. Poor countries, on the other hand, traditionally have been beset by an economically inefficient legal system that undermines their ability to attract private funds. The exception to this rule has been Asia, a region where several countries enjoyed exceptional economic growth even though they lacked the "proper" institutional legal framework. Ginsburg's examination of recent Asia scholarship, in which some studies demonstrate the importance of law to economic prosperity and others do not, concludes that questions about the relationship of law to economic performance remain to be answered (2000). Interestingly, Ginsburg notes that problems related to the lack of effective formal legal institutions may have been reduced in Asia by both the availability of efficient, informal legal instruments and the role of the "developmental state" (2000). Latin America enjoys neither of these advantages.

Latin America's legal institutions, traditionally unable to constrain leaders or to uphold bargains between individuals or firms, have failed to ensure credible property rights commitments. With the transition to a market-led economy, weak legal institutions came to be recognized as a hindrance to investment and a significant structural barrier to growth in the region.[6] In today's conventional wisdom, governments implementing market-based economic reforms must concern themselves with the provision of a legal environment conducive to capitalist economic growth. In particular, international financial institutions (IFIs) have emphasized the need for developing countries to establish legal institutions, via the reform of their judicial structures and legal systems, capable of inducing and protecting private investment.

The Role of International Financial Institutions and Judicial Reform in the Developing World

A near halt of all private lending and other capital inflows to the Third World followed Mexico's 1982 announcement that it could not service its debt, plunging countries throughout the developing world into severe economic crises. In response, these countries sought emergency economic assistance—in the form of new loans—from international financial institutions. However, along with fresh loans came conditionality agreements requiring the implementation of immediate stabilization policies and longer-term structural adjustment programs. As a result, many countries of the developing world undertook dramatic economic reforms, replacing their state-led economies with more market-based policies and a private-sector-led economic model.

While the conditionality agreements signed with international financial institutions in the 1980s concentrated primarily on economic variables, by the early 1990s the IFIs began to focus upon a broader set of "good governance" structural reforms intended to create the proper enabling environment for a market economy to develop and prosper. In consequence, institutional reforms that could protect property rights, such as independent judiciaries and effective legal systems, became priorities.[7] As early as 1991, the World Bank formally noted the need for developing countries to improve their legal infrastructure (World Bank 1991, 9). Two years later, at its 1993 Conference on Judicial Reform in Latin America and the Caribbean (the first of several attended by senior-level political, judicial, and economic representatives and dedicated entirely to judicial reform), the bank stressed the importance of creating "an enabling legal and judicial environment that is conducive to trade, financing, and investment" (Aiyer 1995, vii). The Inter-American Development ment Bank sponsored its own conference, Judicial Reform in the Western Hemisphere, in 1995. By the mid-1990s, the link between judicial improvements and economic reform had become standard fare in the discussion of growth strategies for the developing world, with judicial reform seen as a necessary complement to the purely economic reforms of the previous period (Shihata 1995; Messick 1999). The level of loans, projects, publications, and conferences on Latin American judicial reform sponsored by the IFIs in the last fifteen years demonstrates the degree to which judicial reform has become a primary concern for the region.[8]

While the IFIs cannot outright force developing countries to undertake certain policies, they are able to influence those countries' domestic decision-making processes and to increase the appeal of certain reforms. First, IFIs can signal which types of projects will receive funding, which in turn influences which types of projects will be pursued. Second, IFIs have the ability to influence the availability of funds in these countries more generally. They provide funds directly, whether grants or loans, to cover outstanding debt and engage in new development projects. In addition, the decision of the major IFIs to award or deny a particular country its "stamp of approval" influences inflows of private investment. Hence, IFIs have the ability to structure the dialogue about development and to encourage the pursuit of specific policies.

Latin American countries, after having ignored their judiciaries for decades, jumped on the judicial reform bandwagon in the 1990s. Almost every government declared its intent to undertake major judicial reforms and legal improvements. Did this wave of judicial reform occur as a result of pressures from IFIs and the transition to a market economy?

*Limitations of the Hypotheses Based on IFI Pressures
and the Transition to a Market Economy*

Given the reigning consensus on property rights institutions, governments in the developing world have strong economic incentives, both international and domestic, to engage in judicial reform. However, although these economic pressures influenced the general timing and design of *initiation*, they cannot explain the variations in *implementation* (the key determinant of judicial empowerment) of these reforms. First, as regards external agents, Latin American leaders faced pressures from IFIs to engage in judicial reform, and it is no surprise that as judicial reform came to be a priority for the IFIs, it also emerged as a key issue on the Latin American agenda. The IFIs pushed a "recipe" of policy prescriptions for the judicial sector, and loans were made available for specific types of judicial reforms. These included, for example, the adoption of national judicial councils, the creation of judicial academies, and the establishment of alternative dispute resolution mechanisms. Indeed, the IFIs' general formula for judicial reform has served as a template for most of the reforms initiated in the region.

Critics have argued that Latin American countries have been coerced into undertaking judicial reform out of fear of IFI economic retaliation. The fact that IFIs enjoy influence in the developing world due to their financial leverage cannot be denied. Yet neither the World Bank nor the International Monetary Fund (IMF), the two most influential international agencies involved in economic restructuring, has tied general economic assistance to specific changes in the judicial branch. Indeed, the IMF has not been an active participant in judicial reform; it has not funded any judicial reform programs or withheld funding due to progress on a specific judicial project. As for World Bank funding, neither new structural adjustment loans nor the disbursement of funds for economic reform from existing standing agreements has been linked to judicial independence or progress on judicial reform (Hammergren 1999). Failure to advance on judicial reforms may result in the termination of judicial sector loans, as in Peru in the late 1990s, but it has not resulted in the suspension of general economic assistance.

Interestingly, of the three cases under study here, the successful implementation of judicial reform was inversely correlated with the receipt of an IFI judicial sector loan. Mexico, the only country where judicial restructuring was immediately and meaningfully implemented, did not receive any international funding for its 1994 judicial reforms.[9] As for Argentina, in 1998—four years after that country initiated judicial reform—the country received two IFI loans for judicial reform projects.[10] Indeed, Argentina received financing for judicial projects even though it was evident that the government had been stalling on the implementation of the constitutional reforms that it had initiated in 1994. Furthermore, Argentina's other IFI economic assistance was not affected by its failure to carry through with judicial advancements. Finally, as for Peru, its major institutional judicial reforms, including the 1993 constitutional revisions and several other structural judicial reforms initiated in the mid-1990s, were self-funded. In late 1997 Peru signed a US$22.5 million loan agreement with the World Bank to strengthen the judiciary, but that loan was terminated in September 1998, before it became effective, due to executive intervention in the judiciary. Yet, even given the outright undermining of judicial independence by the Peruvian government, Peru continued to receive IFI economic funding for general restructuring and new development projects. In addition, it is important to note that both of the World Bank loans for Argentina and Peru were negotiated several years after their respective judicial reforms occurred.

In sum, the IFIs have emphasized the need for developing countries to engage in judicial reform, they have provided a package of prescribed institutional changes to serve as a general model for such reform, and they have supplied funding to enact these changes. But the IFIs have proved very lax at monitoring the implementation of judicial reform and have not imposed penalties for failure to carry through with promised institutional advancements. (These ideas are further elaborated in the next section of this chapter.) Hence, pressures from international agencies are important for understanding the initiation of judicial reform in Latin America and the similarity of these proclaimed reforms across borders, but these pressures cannot explain the variations in judicial power resulting from supposedly similar reforms.

Domestic economic pressures, like their international counterparts, serve better as a factor contributing to the demand for judicial reform than as a determinant of its supply. Government leaders who implement economic reforms have an incentive to pursue judicial reform in order to bolster economic performance and improve their chances of remaining in office. In Latin America, the recognition of the link between the judiciary and economic performance has been particularly pronounced. Officials in the region (including presidents and upper-echelon politicians, economic advisers, members of the judiciary, and business representatives) have publicly called for judicial reform to encourage private investment and foster economic growth. In a globalized financial system, developing countries compete against each other (as well as against the industrialized world) to attract private investment. Individual countries can ill afford not to level the playing field against the more secure business environments offered by the first world. Given this powerful incentive to follow through with judicial reform, why have reforms stalled at the initiation stage? Economic arguments fail to explain variations in power of the postreform judiciaries because they overlook the potential political costs implied by judicial reform: a judiciary that is made strong enough to protect economic rights will also be made strong enough to limit the ruling party's authority.

Institutional changes to the judiciary have both *economic* and *political* consequences; the changes to the judiciary necessary to create an efficient legal system are precisely those that would produce a judiciary positioned to play an independent role in the political balance of power. Judicial independence, once established, cannot be restricted to economic issues alone. Thus, presidents and legislators who pursue judicial reform for its economic benefits are likely to increase simultaneously the judiciary's power to check their own ability to pursue preferred policies.[11] The existence of these political costs negatively affects a politician's willingness to engage in judicial reform.

In sum, judicial reform has both potential benefits and potential costs. The countries of Latin America had similar economic incentives for undertaking judicial reform, yet there exists a substantial divergence in how seriously these reforms were pursued. Thus, it becomes evident that the economic benefits alone were not sufficient to induce the ruling political parties in these countries to accept the political costs of judicial reform. Yet in some cases reform was carried out and real power was handed over to the courts. Thus the question arises, under what circumstances will politicians pursue meaningful judicial reform? To answer this question requires an understanding of how political actors weigh the potential costs and benefits of judicial reform, and how this perceived balance may change over time.

A Political Argument to Explain Latin America's Judicial Reforms

Explaining Institutional Reform (in General) and Judicial Empowerment (in Particular)

The recent wave of global democratic transitions has focused attention on the importance of institutions and how these "rules of the game" establish opportunities for, and place constraints upon, political leaders. Conventional political logic holds that political actors should be expected to take action that increases their political power and their chances to maintain it (Ames 1987; Geddes 1995). Generally speaking, ruling parties prefer to minimize constraints upon their exercise of power, while members of the opposition—by definition those who do not hold power—prefer to impose limits on the ability to wield authority. Furthermore, those who possess the power to restructure political institutions will do so if this will enable them to replace existing institutions with those that better serve their interests (North 1990).

Applying these ideas about institutional choice to the judicial branch, ruling parties should prefer a judiciary with a weaker capacity to challenge their political prerogatives, while opposition parties should prefer a judiciary capable of checking unfettered decision making by the ruling party. Extending this logic to judicial reform, ruling parties should not be expected to willfully enact reforms that increase the judiciary's potential to limit the government. On the other hand, members of the opposition should push for increases in judicial autonomy to check presidential and legislative power (since they do not control these) as well as to protect the political rights of the opposition (themselves).

It must be remembered, though, that institutional outcomes are determined not only by the preferences of political players, but also by their capacity to achieve those preferences. If the ruling party is able to implement reform unilaterally, then we should not expect reforms to increase the judiciary's ability to restrain government actions. But if a coalition is required to pass reform, then the game becomes one in which the opposition must be provided with judicial incentives in order to approve the reform. Thus, a constitutional design favoring the development of an empowered judiciary is more likely where there exists at least one opposition party whose vote is necessary for the passage of reform.

The above discussion on institutional reforms, however, reflects a static environment. While it is obvious that political actors take actions to improve their political position in the current time period, it must also be emphasized that they take action with an eye to the future as well; and, where uncertainty exists about a ruling party's future standing in the domestic political arena, intertemporal interests may have significant consequences for the outcome of such reform. Should a ruling party foresee that it may no longer dominate a political system in which it has previously held power, then that ruling party has an incentive to strengthen institutional counterweights that may constrain the use of power by future ruling parties. In such scenarios, it is in a ruling party's interest to make sure that those who come to power in the future will be unable to change the rules of the political game in ways that would be detrimental to the former ruling party. Hence, while a ruling party that expects to remain in power should not be expected to empower the judicial branch, fortifying the judiciary makes sense where a ruling party's chances of remaining in office are decreasing.

Several scholars in the last decade have analyzed the importance of the electoral market upon judicial empowerment. Ramseyer, examining Japanese and U.S. politics, argues that judicial independence is more likely where expectations of continued elected government coincide with political parties' perceptions that their chances of continuous electoral victory are low (1994).[12] Hirschl's work on Israel argues that constitutionalization of rights and the concomitant strengthening of judicial review to enforce these rights is facilitated when judicial fortification serves as a source of "hegemonic preservation": ruling elites, threatened by the emergence of new political bases that undermine their control over majoritarian institutions, may transfer political power to an insulated and empowered judiciary that remains more aligned with their ideological values (2001).[13]

According to Ginsburg, the creation of stronger courts at constitutional conventions gives credibility to constitutional bargains struck by political elites, as leaders perceive that independent courts will uphold prior agreements worked out by constitutional drafters. Analyzing variations in design and power of constitutional courts in emerging democracies in Asia, Ginsburg argues that electoral uncertainty when drafting constitutional courts leads to the establishment of stronger courts (access, review powers, court size, etc.). In addition, the success of the courts in the following period is more likely when the court operates in a more diffuse political space, as such diffusion increases the court's potential allies in ruling against a particular political institution (2003).[14]

In my earlier research on judicial reform in Latin America, I have argued that a ruling party with an uncertain future may decide to increase the independence and authority of the courts to serve as a hedge against possible downturns in its own future political position. Establishing a stronger judicial branch is a source of insurance: it decreases the risks that political elites face should they become the opposition. However, like an insurance policy, such reform implies upfront costs in exchange for future protection. In the current period, the newly empowered court may challenge the very government that oversaw increases in judicial power. While these increases imply potential costs to the ruling political leaders in the short run, they may ultimately serve these actors' long-run interests should these leaders lose their position of political dominance. Precisely because judicial reform entails potential costs, a ruling party should attempt to delay its implementation until an empowered court might serve as protection (2004, 2005).

To apply an institutional argument based on the electoral market to Latin America's judicial reforms in the 1990s, we must first lay out the particular sequencing of the region's judicial reforms. Latin American judicial reforms have not been a one-shot deal; rather they have been a two-stage process of initiation and implementation. Understanding Latin America's judicial reforms will therefore require an analysis of the incentives of political actors at both periods of the judicial reform process.

Latin America's Recent Two-Staged Judicial Reforms:
Initiation and Implementation

In the first stage of judicial reform, the initiation phase, the judicial branch is altered by the passage of constitutional changes. Initiation can be viewed as a "proclamation period" in which coming judicial advancements are formally announced via the rewriting of the national constitution. The second stage of reform, implementation, entails the passage of congressional legislation to translate the newly agreed-upon constitutional principles into a working reality. For example, the rewritten constitution, declaring the goal of judicial independence, may proclaim the creation of a nonpartisan judicial council responsible for appointing all future judges. But only with the passage of legislation will the council be officially established and begin functioning. Until the passage of the implementing legislation, the new constitutional principles remain in limbo.

Equally important, it is often left to the implementing legislation to provide the details that will translate the new, abstract judicial concepts into concrete institutional structures. With respect to judicial councils, for example, these details may specify the number of council members, the selection process for its representatives, or the council's control over lower-level judicial appointments. As for constitutional courts, while the constitution may establish such a court, it may be left to later legislation to clarify the number of justices, the types of issues that may come before the court, or whether a simple or super majority is required to declare a law unconstitutional. Thus, while the promulgation of constitutional changes may declare profound institutional changes and elegant new principles, *it is the details and vigor of the implementing legislation that is crucial in determining the independence and authority of the restructured judicial branch.*

Finally, it must be noted that the political support necessary to pass each phase of reform is distinct. Altering a national constitution generally requires broader political support than passing congressional legislation. In many countries, enacting constitutional changes often requires the approval of at least two-thirds of the members of the national assembly authorized to amend a country's constitution. In effect, the ruling party must form a coalition with at least one opposition party in order to approve constitutional judicial changes. In other cases, the new constitution has to be approved by the public in a national referendum, forcing the ruling party to accede to the preferences of the voting population. In either case, the ruling party is forced to seek allies to pass its reforms. The implementation stage, on the other hand, requires only the approval of a simple majority, a level of congressional support that ruling parties frequently possess. Hence, unlike initiation, implementation of the judicial reforms enshrined in a revised constitution may be overseen by the ruling party acting alone.

Putting It All Together: Latin America's 1990s Two-Staged Judicial Reforms

The fact that Latin America's judicial reforms occurred in two distinct steps, each of which entailed unique costs and benefits, has important ramifications for the development of postreform judiciaries in the region. Specifically, while the initiation of judicial reform has been readily achieved, the implementation of meaningful judicial reform has been much less likely to occur and requires a much more stringent set of conditions.

As for initiations, from the vantage point of the ruling party, the promulgation of constitutional revisions increasing judicial power has two primary benefits: those received in exchange for satisfying the demands of international financial institutions, and those received by using judicial reform as a "bargaining chip" in a political trade. With respect to the former, the initiation of judicial reform allows a government to demonstrate progress on IFI-sponsored structural adjustment programs. In consequence, the initiating country is awarded a "stamp of approval," facilitating economic inflows from international agencies.

The second set of major benefits comes from the use of judicial reform in political trades. This is because constitutional changes often require the approval of at least two-thirds of a constitutional assembly, a level of support that ruling parties have usually lacked. Thus, in order to obtain institutional reforms that they were seeking and could not achieve unilaterally, ruling parties may be willing to entice the opposition to agree to this change by offering to increase the checking power of other political institutions. While the judiciary traditionally enjoyed little political currency in Latin America, in the 1990s the judicial branch came to be seen as a valuable bargaining chip in deals involving institutional reform. Ruling parties appeared willing to cede improvements to the national judiciary in exchange for other institutional reforms that the ruling party could not otherwise achieve.

The preceding paragraphs have outlined a range of economic and political benefits, benefits that were both specific and immediate, which the ruling party could enjoy as a result of the initiation of judicial reform.[15] But along with these benefits, it must be remembered that initiation also entails a potential cost: specifically, the possibility of judicial interference with the ruling party's exercise of authority. However, at the first stage of reform, *this cost is delayed.* Only after implementation does the ruling party incur the cost of judicial reform. Thus, in the view of the ruling party, though the rewards of judicial reform are instant and specific at initiation, at that time its costs are *neither immediate nor certain.*

The opposition also perceives benefits from the initiation of judicial reform: an independent judiciary is viewed as protection against potential abuses of power committed by the ruling party. Because its support is often needed to pass constitutional changes, the opposition is able to modify the ruling party's proposed constitutional reforms in the direction of greater judicial power. As for the costs of reform, these are incurred only if the judicial reform is part of a trade in which the opposition agrees to empower an institution controlled by the ruling party. However, the opposition is amenable to such institutional exchanges because it believes that the reformed judiciary will be a powerful counterweight to the branches of government (controlled by the ruling party) being strengthened.

In sum, both the ruling party and the opposition must agree to initiate judicial reform, and, at this stage, both parties can agree to constitutional changes that empower the judicial branch. Consequently, initiation is easy to attain. Initiation, however, is just half of the judicial reform story.

Implementation, the crucial second stage in the judicial reform process, has proved much more difficult to achieve. This is because the ruling party's perceptions of the costs and benefits of reform do not necessarily remain fixed between the initiation and implementation periods. In contrast, the opposition's preferences remain constant over both periods.[16] But while the opposition's preferences remain fixed from initiation to implementation, during the second stage its bargaining strength decreases dramatically as its support is no longer required. It is the ruling party that unilaterally controls the second stage of reform, yet at this stage of reform the ruling party often lacks incentives to see it through.

Two factors converge to alter the ruling party's perceived value of reform from the initiation to the implementation stage. On one hand, the benefits to be obtained by the ruling party by continuing forward with judicial reform have decreasing returns. First, the IFIs have not offered additional economic assistance for progress on implementation, nor have they imposed serious penalties for nonimplementation. In fact, they have proved unable, or unwilling, to monitor progress on implementation.[17] In addition, the benefits gained from a judicial trade are exhausted at the time the new constitution is enacted. For example, if the president obtains the right to re-election in exchange for constitutional increases in judicial power, the president may still enjoy his second term even without implementing these promised judicial reforms.

On the other hand, the costs of judicial reform, which remain only potential costs at initiation, become concrete realities if reform is implemented. For the ruling party, following through with judicial reform means accepting limits on its political power. The ruling party would have to play by the rules; and it would be the courts, not the ruling party, that would decide what those rules were and where they were trespassed. Thus, while the benefits of moving from initiation to implementation do not increase, the costs for doing so are exceptionally high. As a result, initiated reforms are often stymied at implementation.

Yet despite the severe costs of following through with reform, in some instances judicial reforms are fully implemented. Given the high costs associated with implementation, and the limited benefits, why would politicians from the ruling party ever undertake the second stage of reform? As argued earlier, implementation of judicial reforms makes sense as an insurance policy under a particular set of circumstances. Where a ruling party's probability of remaining in office is low, the ruling party may seek the implementation of judicial advancements. Should the ruling party become the opposition, an independent judiciary can limit the capacity of the incoming politicians to change the rules of the game in ways that may hinder the former ruling party from returning to power (for example, altering electoral rules or campaign finance laws). It also limits the capacity of incoming politicians to undermine policies established by the outgoing ruling party. A judiciary capable of constraining ruling parties, the outcome associated with meaningful implementation of judicial reform, may come to be seen as a benefit rather than a cost.

In sum, the real cost of implementing judicial reform is not fixed; rather, it depends on the ruling party's perception of retaining political power. As the chances of losing power increase, motivation to implement agreed-upon judicial advancements should also increase. Hence, the likelihood of meaningful implementation of judicial reform increases as the ruling party's probability of retaining political office declines. We should expect the implementation of positive judicial reform to be closely connected to elections in which the ruling party appears likely to cede its position of political dominance.

Conclusion

While economic pressures can help explain the timing and similarity of Latin America's constitutional judicial reform packages, the significant variation in implementation of reform cannot be explained by economic arguments alone. Economic rewards are just one aspect of a politician's view of judicial reform, and these rewards are usually outweighed by the high political costs implied by the full implementation of judicial reform.

A complete explanation of Latin America's judicial reform requires a disaggregation of judicial reform so as to analyze political incentives at both stages of the reform process. The initiation of judicial reform provides benefits to opposition and ruling parties alike and is therefore relatively easy to achieve. However, the real power of postreform courts depends on implementation, and it is the ruling party that retains discretion over this stage of reform. And from the ruling party's perspective, the convergence of decreasing benefits and increasing costs at implementation results in the erosion of the ruling party's will to carry through with promised reforms. For politicians to proceed with implementation, they must perceive political gains that offset political costs. This is most likely where the ruling party faces an uncertain political environment and judicial empowerment serves as political insurance. Hence, the creation of a powerful judiciary, via the meaningful implementation of judicial reform, is most likely where the ruling party perceives it is unlikely to retain its control over political power.

Chapter Two

Judicial Reform in Argentina in the 1990s

Argentina's tumultuous twentieth-century political history has been marked by a weak and subservient judiciary that has traditionally served to uphold laws passed by illegitimate civil and military governments alike. Beset by chronic instability and repeated replacement, the Argentine Supreme Court has been unable to develop the institutional independence or the political will required to challenge the prevailing leadership.[1] "Indeed, almost every new government has had a judiciary of its own choice. For example, during the military regimes, one of the first acts was to assault judicial power (Stotzky and Nino 1993, 12). In fact, rather than serve as a check on authority, the Supreme Court acquiesced in the expansion of executive power (Nino 1993, 326–27). Given the historic impotence of the Argentine judiciary, when Argentina returned to democratic rule in 1983 there existed little expectation that the country's Supreme Court would emerge as a subject of keen academic interest. Nor was there any reason to believe that the judicial apparatus would take center stage in the political struggle over the restructuring of the country's political institutions. Yet in the last decade the Argentine judiciary became the focus of much scholarly literature examining judicial independence and behavior (Helmke 2002; Iaryczower, Spiller, and Tomassi 2002; and Bill-Chavez 2003).[2] Furthermore, control of the judicial branch emerged as a key bargaining chip in the rewriting of the Argentine constitution.

More specifically, Argentina's 1994 judicial reform, included as part of a larger package of constitutional reforms, was a negotiated deal between the country's two most important political parties, the Peronists and the Radicals. In exchange for the right to re-election, Argentina's Peronist president Carlos Menem agreed to Radical Party demands to swap the "ownership" of the Supreme Court (which Menem had packed four years earlier) and to establish a national judicial council to increase the independence of lower-level federal judges. However, after Menem's successful re-election bid in 1995, the president failed to recompose the Supreme Court and used his control of Congress to delay the creation of the council. It was only when it appeared that the Peronists would not retain control of the presidency in 1999 that the president finally relinquished control over the judicial branch. In the Argentine case, I argue that while the ruling Peronist Party could be induced in 1994 to *initiate* reforms, the Peronists then proved unwilling to *implement* these changes until they believed that they were likely to lose their position of political power.

The first section of this chapter discusses the Argentine judiciary in the decade following the 1983 return to civilian rule. The next section describes the Radical-Peronist political trades that provided the foundation for Argentina's 1994 constitutional reform. The next two sections detail the initiation and implementation phases of Argentina's reform, respectively. The final section uses my argument to explain Argentina's experience with judicial reform.

The Argentine Judiciary, 1983–1994

The Return to Democracy and Judicial Independence, 1983–1989

In 1983, after seven years of repressive military rule, Argentina returned to democracy with free and fair elections. While Argentina's political history has long been shaped by the alternation of civil and military regimes, the juntas that governed the country between 1976 and 1983 had been exceptionally brutal, with the military responsible for the "disappearance" of an estimated thirty thousand people, as well as numerous acts of torture, kidnapping, and murder. Argentina's new president, Raul Alfonsín of the Radical Party, was a human rights lawyer who campaigned on a platform committed to democratization and the search for justice, two issues that resounded strongly with the Argentine public. Argentina's newly elected leadership was particularly concerned that individual rights be protected under the civilian government and that former military leaders be held accountable for the systematic violation of human rights committed under their rule.

Hence, just three days after coming to office, Alfonsín declared that legal action would be taken against military officials for the massive human rights violations committed during their rule. He immediately initiated legislation to nullify the "Self-Amnesty Law" decreed by the junta prior to yielding power. The law pardoned all acts of military violence between 1976 and 1983. Alfonsín's actions enjoyed the support of both the legislature and the judiciary, with Congress promulgating the law shortly after its introduction and the Supreme Court later upholding it in a 1983 decision.[3] While the trials would remain severely limited, and in fact only nine individuals were sentenced, it was "the first time since the breakdown of democracy in 1930 that authoritarian rulers must answer for their actions before a court of law" (Waisman 1989, 102).[4] Alfonsín also established the Commission for Disappeared Persons to investigate and document all alleged abuses committed under military rule, and introduced a proposal to reform Argentina's Military Justice Code.[5] Thus, at the start of his presidential term Alfonsín appeared committed to delivering on his human rights campaign promises.

Another of Alfonsín's early acts in office was to fill the newly vacated Supreme Court. Days prior to Alfonsín's inauguration, the five-member Argentine Supreme Court voluntarily resigned *en masse* to allow the emerging democracy to start fresh with "untainted" justices. The ideological and party affiliations of Alfonsín's five nominees covered the political spectrum and possessed admirable academic and professional qualifications. Three were associated with different branches of the Radical Party, one was a Socialist, and the other a traditional Peronist.[6] Interestingly, the naming of the new court sparked little political debate, media attention, or public interest. For example, announcement of the new justices merited only five short paragraphs in the country's most prestigious paper, with the article listing only the name, age, education, and specialty of each prospective justice (*La Nación* 1983). Indeed, the public was much more interested in the naming of judges to the Federal

Courts of Appeal (the civilian courts that were to investigate allegations of human rights violations by the military) than they were in the naming of the Supreme Court justices (Verbitsky 1993, 20).

Paralleling the public's lack of interest in the membership of Argentina's highest judicial organ, political elites from both major parties appeared equally unconcerned with the composition of the Supreme Court. The Peronist-controlled Senate, whose support was required to approve the justices, readily confirmed the Radical's three-member majority on the court. As for the Radicals, Alfonsín initially offered the position of chief justice to the Peronists' presidential candidate, Italo Luder, whom Alfonsín had just defeated. Rather than viewing this as an honor, Luder perceived the gesture as "a way of emphasizing Alfonsín's electoral victory and placing Luder in a position of minor relevance" and refused the position (Oteiza 1994, 111). Clearly, in 1983 there existed little expectation by either party or by the public at large that the court would emerge as an important political player.

The Argentine judiciary, although not all-powerful during the post-democratization period, was independent and enjoyed a broad scope of authority (Larkins 1998, 427). The court's vision of its place in Argentine politics was summed up by its new Supreme Court chief justice, Gemaro Carrio: "The Supreme Court must recover the role that it is destined to play in the governmental system in our country, to safeguard the supremacy of the constitution and exercise checks on the other powers" (Oteiza 1994, 103). In fact, the court's liberal interpretation of the law under the Alfonsín administration led to an unprecedented expansion of individual rights and guarantees (see Bacque 1995). On average the court ruled against the government 37 percent of the time between 1983 and 1987 (Helmke 2002, 296). During the final two years of Alfonsín's presidency, antigovernment rulings increased to an average of 47 percent of all judicial decisions (Helmke 2002, 296). In particular, the court effectively blocked some of the president's emergency economic measures.

The court, however, was not the only challenge confronting Alfonsín in the second half of his six-year term. The president was also beset by crises on the military and economic fronts. By this time, investigations of human rights violations were targeting active-duty members of the military, rather than high-ranking officers who were already retired. Low morale and uprisings in the barracks in 1986 and 1987 had the Alfonsín administration anxious about a possible coup attempt. In response, the government passed two laws, effectively stopping all human rights trials (the Final Stop Law of December 1986 and the Law of Due Obedience in June 1987).[7] In addition, despite the Radicals' numerous emergency measures, Argentina was experiencing severe economic deterioration. Both the sacrifice of human rights concerns and the continuing downward economic spiral led to widespread disillusionment with the Alfonsín administration which hurt the Radicals at the polls.

While the Radicals faired poorly in the 1987 October midterm elections, the Peronists were able to capitalize on the Radicals' diminishing political standing. The Peronists increased their representation in Argentina's Congress and also picked up seventeen state governorships, including the powerful position of governor of the state of Buenos Aires. Alfonsín, realizing he would need bipartisan support to achieve any of his goals, met with the newly elected governor of Buenos Aires to exchange ideas about ways to confront the country's economic crisis in November 1987. The following January the two men signed a document in which they agreed to establish a bipartisan commission to study possible constitutional reforms.

At the same time, both the Radicals and the Peronists were beginning to demonstrate an interest in adding members to the Supreme Court. The Argentine constitution, like that of the United States, does not specify the number of justices to sit on the court; instead this is determined by ordinary congressional legislation. Hence, altering the number of justices does not require a difficult constitutional amendment process in Argentina (or in the United States); rather, it may be achieved merely with the support of a simple majority in Congress. As a result of the midterm elections, any deal to enlarge the court would require the support of Peronists in the upper house. While the Radicals proposed adding two members to the court, the Peronists' counteroffer sought to increase the number of justices by four.[8] Although the court packing failed, as the two sides proved unable to reach an agreement on the precise number of justices to be added, the attempt demonstrates the dramatic reversal of political interest in the court since Argentina's return to civilian rule just a few years prior.

While the two main parties could not agree on changes to the court, they did begin to make progress on some issues of constitutional reforms and released a joint document expressing general areas of agreement in the fall of 1988.[9] The document proposed incorporating greater protection of individual rights in the new constitution, but otherwise made no mention of reforming the judiciary or modifying its institutional structure. This trend of limited concern for institutional judicial reform continued with each party's 1989 campaign platform: the Radicals omitted the judiciary entirely, and the Peronists included only a very general statement calling for increased judicial independence, efficiency, and objectivity.

Menem and the Loss of Judicial Independence:
The Argentine Judiciary 1989–1994

In Argentina's 1989 national elections, the Peronists swept Congress and their presidential candidate, Carlos Menem, won the presidency. Amid a deepening economic crisis, which forced Alfonsín to step down, Menem took office early. In stark contrast to his campaign promises, the newly inaugurated president embarked on an orthodox economic program, which he implemented by relying on Argentina's system of tight party discipline in Congress and by liberally availing himself of a (questionable) right to declare "Decrees of Necessity and Urgency."[10] Menem's presidency would prove to be defined by an increasing concentration of power in the hands of the executive, at the expense of other governmental institutions, as he aggressively pursued his economic and political goals.

The Argentine Supreme Court, however, unlike the Peronist-controlled Congress, did not appear amenable to either the president's economic program or his centralization of authority. According to the legal columnist for *La Nación,* "Menem knew that the Court was not going to make itself compliant" (Ventura 1999).[11] During his presidential campaign, Menem had publicly promised not to intervene in the court, and he had also affirmed these sentiments in private meetings with the justices (Verbitsky 1993, 36). After Menem won the presidential election, however, packing the court became his preferred solution to the looming constraint of real judicial oversight. Shortly before the president's inauguration, "members of Menem's inner circle reportedly offered ambassadorships and other prestigious posts to various Justices in order to induce their resignations, thereby giving the new president a few vacancies to fill" (Larkins 1998, 426). When that strategy failed to bear fruit, Menem opted for a more proactive approach.

In September 1989 Menem sent a proposal to Congress to add four justices to the Supreme Court.[12] The sitting justices, as well as the Radicals in Congress, immediately voiced their vehement opposition to the president's attempt to stack the court. But as the action was not prohibited by the Argentine constitution, they could not prevent it from becoming law. Readily approved by the Peronist-controlled Senate, it was passed, under a questionable quorum, in the lower house on April 5, 1990.[13] Given that the selection process for justices relied on a simple Senate majority, and that the Peronists controlled the Senate, Menem was able to handpick the four new justices. The chief justice resigned in protest, and as a result Menem was able to personally designate five of the nine members on the court. On April 18 Menem sent the names of five Supreme Court candidates to the Senate for confirmation. The list was ratified the following day, after only six minutes of debate, and the new justices assumed their posts a week later. Shortly thereafter another Alfonsín-appointed justice resigned from the court in protest, his replacement raising the tally of Menem-appointed justices on the Supreme Court to six.

These "Menemista" justices possessed either close personal ties to the president and/or a conservative legal philosophy with respect to the role of the judiciary. New Supreme Court chief justice Julio Nazareno was Menem's former law partner in the state of La Rioja and had been the state's Supreme Court chief justice when Menem was the La Rioja governor. Besides Nazareno, the new justices were Eduardo Moline O'Conner, Mariano Carvagno Martínez, Rudolfo Barra, Ricardo Levene, and Julio Oyhanarte. Vice Chief Justice Moline O'Conner was the brother-in-law of two of Menem's close advisers (as well as his doubles tennis partner), and Justice Carvagno Martínez was a close friend of Menem's brother (Baglini and D'Ambrosio 1993, 78–82). Justice Barra, upon learning of his nomination to the court, stated, "My only two bosses are Peron and Menem" (Verbitsky 1993, 56), and later declared in an interview with *Pagina 12* that the role of the Supreme Court was "to go along with the politics of the president."[14]

The new justices, serving both to facilitate and legitimate the president's policies, provided for a dramatically different court majority.[15] According to law professor Alberto Dalla Via, the court demonstrated a "clear policy of accompanying the government" (Dalla Via 1999). A brief glance at the voting record of important cases readily confirms this point. Decisions favoring the government were characteristically six-to-three majority opinions, with all six Menem-appointed justices voting in concert (Verbitsky 1993, 135). The Argentine Supreme Court, following its brief period of independence between 1983 and 1989, became tied to the government once again after its packing in 1990.

Paralleling the experience of Argentina's high court, lower levels of the Argentine judiciary were also subject to severe executive intervention in the 1990s. A 1991 reform of the country's penal code nearly doubled the number of federal judges, and these newly created posts were packed with Menem appointees. In 1992 Menem's minister of justice abruptly resigned, claiming that Menem's process of judicial selection was "undermining attempts to create an independent legal system" (*Latin American Research Review—Southern Cone* 1992, 2). Menem also elevated many first-instance judges to the appellate level and then appointed his own judges to fill the vacated first-instance posts. Thus, as these first-instance judges often determine whether a case should be thrown out, the president ensured himself a "filter" to terminate cases at the first rung of the judicial ladder (Ventura 1999).

Under Menem, judicial constraints were effectively abolished, and the short-lived era of the courts as active participants in the Argentine system of checks and balances came to an abrupt end. Lower-level judgeships were filled with the president's nominees, and the Menemista court served as an "enabler" of the president's economic programs and political goals. Thus, when Menem began actively to seek presidential re-election via constitutional reform—and discovered to his chagrin that he could not attain this goal without the support of the Radicals—the latter already had in mind the precise changes they would demand in exchange for their support.

Argentina's 1994 Constitutional Reform: Presidential Re-election in Exchange for Institutional Checks on Executive Power

Prior to 1994, the Argentine constitution prohibited a president from serving a consecutive term. As early as April 1990, less than a year after coming to power, Menem publicly expressed his interest in amending the constitution to allow himself a second presidential bid (*La Nación* 1990a). The Peronists, buoyed by their successes in the 1991 midterm elections, began actively pursuing the removal of the constitutional proscription on immediate re-election. However, the Argentine constitution may be amended only by a national convention convoked specifically for that purpose, and this, in turn, requires passage of a special congressional "declaratory law." Unlike ordinary legislation requiring simple majorities in both houses, enactment of this type of special legislation requires the support of two-thirds of the members of each chamber. Menem could readily obtain the necessary two-thirds support to pass a declaratory law in the Senate. But without the support of the Radicals in the Chamber of Deputies, it was unclear whether he could garner this proportion in the lower house.

The Radicals themselves had initially proposed legalizing consecutive presidential re-election after their strong showing in the 1985 midterm election. However, as their political fortunes waned in the second half of the 1980s, so did their interest in legalizing re-election, and they now vociferously opposed Menem's call for a constitutional convention. Victor Martínez, Radical vice president under Alfonsín, wrote in June 1992 a scathing editorial decrying Menem's call to modify the country's founding political document (Martínez 1992). The following month, the Radical Party formally declared its opposition to a constitutional reform, declaring it a blatant re-election ploy that would only exacerbate the ills of Argentina's chronic hyperpresidentialism.[16] At this point, the Radicals appeared unwilling to accede to Menem's plans. And the Peronists, with their confidence running high, decided to await the results of the 1993 lower house midterm election before determining how they would proceed.

As the Peronists had correctly anticipated, the October 1993 election increased their total number of seats in the lower house, doing so at the expense of the Radicals' representatives. Yet even after the election, the Peronists still lacked a solid two-thirds of the vote needed to approve the declaratory law in the Chamber of Deputies. Given that his hopes for presidential re-election depended on the call for a constitutional convention, Menem was unwilling to risk a vote on the bill without complete assurance that it would pass.[17] Thus, for the Peronists the best strategy was to strike a deal with the Radicals and obtain their guaranteed support for a constitutional convention. As for the Radicals after their October electoral defeat, although they retained a hard-line stance against constitutional revisions in public, in private Alfonsín began to engage in a series of secret meetings with Menem to discuss possible options for constitutional reform.

The Senate easily approved a declaratory law at the end of October 1993 and sent the bill on to the Chamber of Deputies. In order to facilitate the law's passage there, Menem threatened to call a national plebiscite on constitutional reforms. With opinion polls indicating that 70 percent of the population would vote in favor of rewriting the constitution (García-Lema 1994, 135), Menem was well aware that the Radicals could ill afford to appear as an obstacle to the popular will. The threat of a plebiscite had its desired effect: on November 14, one week prior to the scheduled referendum, Menem and Alfonsín signed the Acuerdo de Olivos, a bipartisan pact calling for a constitutional convention.

The Acuerdo, later formalized as a package of thirteen areas of institutional reform known as the "Nucleus of Basic Agreements," served as the basis for negotiations between the two parties. On the Peronist side, Menem's primary goal was to obtain the right to run again in the October 1995 presidential election.[18] As for the Radicals, Alfonsín sought to ensure that his party would be able to exercise checks on a re-elected Menem; hence, Alfonsín sought to increase Radical control over institutions that could serve as counterweights to executive power. Specifically, the Radicals demanded: a reduction in presidential tenure from six to four years; increases in judicial independence; creation of a cabinet chief of staff responsible to both the president and Congress; direct election of the mayor of Buenos Aires; an increase in the number of Senate seats awarded to the opposition; and creation of an auditor general's office under the leadership of the major opposition party.

Each of the institutional changes demanded by the Radicals was designed to increase limits on executive power while simultaneously bolstering their own party's political position. The decreased tenure would leave Menem with a shortened second term and would also allow the Radicals a chance to retake the presidential palace in just four years instead of six. With respect to judicial independence, the Radicals sought to free the judicial branch from executive control. (The judicial trades are detailed in the next section.) The chief of staff would be responsible to

Congress as well as to the president, thereby granting some influence to the Radical Party in the legislature. The position of Buenos Aires mayor was then held by a Peronist appointed by Menem, and the Radicals expected to win this post in an open election. As for the increase in senators, the Radicals expected to lose four senators in the next congressional election. By creating a third Senate seat per district, reserved for the top vote-gathering opposition candidate, the Radicals believed they would gain eight additional Senate seats and hoped to break the Peronists' two-thirds hold on the Senate. Finally, the Auditor General's Office, while under the executive branch, would be under Radical leadership. Along with these formal constitutional changes, the Radicals also demanded an informal, "extraconstitutional" judicial change: the transfer of ownership of the court. The Radicals made it clear that support for constitutional reform would not be forthcoming without changes in the composition of the membership of Argentina's Supreme Court.

The solidification of this pact of formal and informal agreements culminated with the Radicals' voting to approve the declaratory law in Argentina's lower house in late December 1993. The law mandated the convocation of a constitutional assembly in spring 1994 and specified the convention's debate procedures and voting rules. The Nucleus of Basic Agreements would be voted on as a "closed packet," thereby forcing the assembly to approve or reject the package of reforms in its entirety.[19] In this way, the Radicals and Peronists intended to bind each other to their agreed-upon promises. In addition, only a simple majority of representatives would be required to approve constitutional revisions, thereby ensuring that the Radicals and Peronists (who together would hold more than half the seats in the assembly) would not have to bargain with other parties.[20] Thus, regardless of the presence of other political parties at the convention, Argentina's 1994 constitution was rewritten by the Radicals and Peronists alone.

Initiation of Judicial Reform in Argentina

Judicial trades, negotiated in the fall of 1993, were pivotal to Argentina's 1994 constitutional reform. This section details both the informal and formal judicial bargains: "ownership" of the court, and decreased executive influence in the judicial branch.

The Informal Agreement: Swapping the Supreme Court

While the Acuerdo had made no mention of the replacement of justices on the court, the topic was discussed widely in the days immediately following the signing of the agreement, as "the press began to juggle the possibility that the Radicals were propagating changes in the membership of the nation's Supreme Court of Justice" (García-Lema 1994, 135). In fact, prior to the signing of the November 1993 Acuerdo, Alfonsín's top negotiators had privately informed Menem's inner circle that the process of constitutional reform could be accelerated if "Menem's administration would be willing to concede increased Radical participation in the Court, and greater control in the naming and obligations of judges" (Balzan 1993a, 20). Ricardo Gil Lavedra, the Radicals' principal negotiator, publicly stated, "The Court, how it is now, is an important obstacle for any agreement," and emphasized that constitutional reform could occur only if there existed sufficient Supreme Court guarantees that the new constitution would be respected (García-Lema 1994, 135).

Menem, on the other hand, initially appeared to be uninterested in altering the court, claiming that he was not only constitutionally barred from seeking the removal of Supreme Court justices, but that this would also constitute a violation of Argentina's separation of powers. A November 22 article confirmed that "the government is not considering 'inducing' changes in the membership of the Supreme Court, even though the Radicals continue to demand it as a necessary and prior condition before [they] will approve any constitutional reform project including reelection" (Balzan 1993b, 22). Yet shortly thereafter, one of Menem's primary negotiators, Carlos Corach, announced that if any member of the court should see fit to step down, "his resignation would be considered a patriotic gesture" (*La Nación* 1993b, 1). Meanwhile, in the Chamber of Deputies, representatives from both the Peronist and Radical parties also began calling for justices to resign (*Clarín* 1993a, 5).

While the two parties had fleshed out the Nucleus of Basic Agreements by the end of November 1993, the Radicals made it clear that they were unwilling to support the declaratory law in the December lower house vote without a renaming of the court. As the Radicals' December 3 internal convention approached (where they were to decide whether they would approve the declaratory law's passage), Alfonsín's spokesman, Simon Lazara, stated, "We are insisting that some members of the Court should go, and if the situation isn't resolved before December 3, then the reform pact could evaporate" (*La Nación* 1993a, 1). On December 1, the first Menem-appointed Supreme Court justice resigned. Two days later, with the Radical convention already under way, a second "Mene-mista" justice announced his immediate resignation and another Menem-appointed justice stated his intention to step down at the end of February.[21] Thus, there was now a total of three vacancies to be filled, and as long as two of them were filled by "non-Menemistas," the government would lose its court majority. In consequence, the Radical National Convention decided that, as long as they could achieve an acceptable agreement with the Peronists on the justices' replacements, they would approve the declaratory law when it came up for a vote in the lower house later that month (*Clarín* 1993b, 5).

Finally, on December 12, the two parties came to an agreement on the naming of the three new justices. Their agreement explicitly identified which incoming justice would fill the seat of each outgoing member of the court.[22] Two of the new justices were from the Radical Party and the third was a Peronist.[23] One Radical and the Peronist were assigned to replace the justices who had already resigned, and the other Radical would replace the third justice who had announced his February departure. According to Humberto Quiroga Lavie, a member of the 1994 constitutional assembly, "It is shameful to remember it, but, what is certain, is that we are talking about a political intervention into the judiciary" (Quiroga Lavie 1999). Argentina's Supreme Court, with six of nine justices favoring Menem, was now to be split five to four favoring the Radical Party. Having achieved this understanding, Menem and Alfonsín signed a formal agreement the following day which finalized all negotiations and confirmed the convocation of a constitutional convention.

*The Formal Constitutional Changes: Supreme Court Selection and
the National Judicial Council*

Argentina's 1994 constitution included important institutional changes that had the potential to reduce executive influence in the judiciary. These changes included a modification of the selection process for Supreme Court justices and the establishment of a national judicial council. First, the new constitution modified appointment procedures for Supreme Court justices. The president would still be responsible for the nomination of Supreme Court candidates, but now their confirmation would require the support of two-thirds of the Senate rather than only a simple majority.[24] This increased the likelihood that future presidents would need the support of at least one other party to ratify their nominees, thereby decreasing the ability of executives to unilaterally name justices.

Second, Argentina's 1994 constitutional reform created a national judicial council responsible for judicial selection and administration below the Supreme Court.[25] In the past, first-instance and appellate-level federal judges had been chosen by the president and confirmed by the Senate. Now the council would conduct written exams for posted judicial openings, and the names of the top three candidates would be forwarded to the executive. The president would then select one name from the slate to send to the Senate for confirmation. As for judicial discipline, the council would be responsible for the initiation of proceedings to investigate alleged judicial misconduct and for the establishment of a special "magistrates jury" to determine sanctions. With respect to the changes in judicial administration (previously under the Supreme Court), the council would control the judicial budget, determine internal regulations, and establish standards to improve judicial education and training.

The creation of a judicial council, however, does not in itself ensure judicial independence. For a council to achieve this goal, it must be independent, and this depends on the method of selecting its members. The Radicals wanted to have the council's composition clearly specified in the new constitution to make sure the appointment of its members would guarantee its independence, but they were unsuccessful in this bid (Quiroga Lavie 1999). Instead, the 1994 constitution left the membership unspecified, stipulating only that the council was to be "chosen periodically, with an equilibrium of representation from the political branches, judges from all instances, and members from the legal community." In addition, the constitution stipulated that the council was to be operational by August 1995, one year after the revised constitution's promulgation. In the interim, the president would remain empowered to name judges.

In sum, along with a package of other institutional reforms, the constitutional convention included both an implicit Supreme Court swap and an explicit set of institutional reforms affecting the judicial branch. The promulgation of the 1994 constitution signaled the completion of the initiation phase of Argentina's judicial reform. At that time, it appeared that the Supreme Court's new majority would be an effective check on the president and that Argentina was embarking on a new era of decreased executive intervention in the judicial branch.

The Implementation of Judicial Reform Under Menem, 1995–1999

In the May 1995 national election, Menem won his re-election bid, and the Peronists continued to control the Senate. With the help of smaller provincial parties, the Peronists could control the Chamber of Deputies as well. Thus, it would be up to Menem's second administration to oversee, or to block, the implementation phase of Argentina's judicial reform.

The Supreme Court Swap

Due to the less than democratic nature of Argentina's 1994 Supreme Court swap, the bargain was never officially included in the preconstitutional documents signed by the two parties, nor was it formalized in any way at the constitutional convention. Thus, in February 1994, when the Peronist justice Ricardo Levene (whose seat was to be given to the Radical Hector Masnatta) did not retire as previously announced, the Radicals found that they possessed no way to enforce their "gentleman's agreement." Menem, enjoying his majority on the court, did not pursue the matter. Thus, when the new constitution was promulgated, Menem both received the right to re-election and retained his influence on the court.

In the first national election under Argentina's new constitution in October 1995, Menem won his re-election bid and the Peronists continued to control both houses of Congress. One month later, when the aging Justice Levene finally resigned on November 27, 1995, the Radicals insisted that the post be offered to Masnatta, the original intended recipient of the seat. Menem did offer the position to Masnatta, but he was no longer available, as Menem had appointed him to a prestigious position at the United Nations' office in Vienna. Thus, upon Masnatta's refusal, Menem offered the position to Adolfo Vazquez, who immediately accepted the post on the afternoon of November 28. When asked why he was selected, Vazquez replied, "Because I am a friend of Menem's" (Grana 1999). Vazquez's personal ties to Menem, and his public expression of his wholehearted belief in the president's economic policies, left little doubt about where his future vote would lie.

However, once Vazquez was nominated, he still had to be confirmed. As a result of the modification of Senate confirmation procedures, approval of the president's nominee would require the support of two-thirds of the Senate. In the October election, as a result of the new "additional" senators, the Radicals had increased their number of members in the upper house, and once they were sworn in, in mid-December, they would break Menem's two-thirds vote bloc in the Senate. Initially, the Peronists announced that the vote on Vazquez's confirmation would take place after December 10, when the Senate's new representatives had already taken office (*La Nación* 1995, 18). But in violation of the Senate's official rules of operation (the regulations mandated a lapse of seven working days between a vote and its introduction on the floor), the Peronists called for an early vote. "The government was not going to risk losing the necessary fifth vote to maintain control over the court and called for an early vote" (Ventura 1995, 9). With the help of several provincial parties, Vazquez, who would prove to be the "most obsequious member of the Court, responding directly to Menem" (Pellet Lastra 1999), was confirmed on December 7 as the court's ninth justice.

With the December 1995 ratification of Vazquez, Menem continued to enjoy a Menemista Supreme Court. The president's hand-picked five-member bloc repeatedly lined up in his favor, with decisions often coming down as a five-to-four split.[26] For example, an article discussing a court ruling that declared the president's decree privatizing airports to be constitutional stated, "As *La Nación* anticipated three weeks ago, the judges that always vote in favor of the government (five of nine) once again gave the go ahead to their boss" (*La Nación* 1997a). Throughout Menem's second term, the Radicals continued to demand an alteration in Supreme Court membership, but to no avail. The court, as it was constituted, served Menem's interests: first, because while he was president his court majority could support his policy goals; and second, because once he was no longer in office, the court could serve to protect Menem's established policies as well as protect the president himself in any future investigation into activities that had transpired during his administration.[27] Menem may have been willing to offer up his control over the court to gain re-election, but once the benefits of agreeing to the exchange were used up, he was no longer interested in accepting the political costs of fulfilling his half of the bargain.

The National Judicial Council

While the constitution proclaimed the creation of this new institution in Article 114, secondary congressional legislation was required before the National Judicial Council could become a working reality. The legislation would define the council's composition, confirm its new members, and fill in the details (for example, the number of council members required to achieve a quorum). According to the 1994 constitution, the new Judicial Council was to be operational by August 24, 1995. During the period between the signing of the 1994 constitution and the creation of the council sometime before August 1995, the president would remain empowered to name judges. But as 1994 passed, the council was not formally discussed in the Menem-controlled Congress. Menem's re-election in May 1995 brought little change, and although a bill was introduced in a Senate committee, it languished there unaddressed. Since an autonomous council could begin appointing independent judges, Menem was in no rush to establish it. In fact, at a meeting with Argentine appellate court judges, Menem declared that "the law sanctioning the [council] was a project to debate for four years" (Ventura 1998a, 268).

According to Humberto Quiroga Lavie, a representative at Argentina's constitutional convention (and future council member), "The Peronists had accepted the Council easily, but became worried when it came time to define it and then they wanted to weaken it" (Quiroga Lavie 1999). A second government council proposal, drafted by Menem's minister of justice, sought to create a twenty-three-member council, thirteen of whom would vote in line with the president (*La Nación* 1996b, 10). The

Senate passed the proposal in March 1996 and sent it to the Chamber of Deputies. Although Menem could enjoy a slight majority in the lower house when working with smaller parties (130 of 257 seats), he could not guarantee that this bill would pass. In particular, the Radicals in the Chamber of Deputies strongly opposed the government's intent to secure a majority on the council. The two parties "maintained a fierce fight over the final composition of the council, as the idea of the Peronists [was] to include enough representatives from the executive branch to assure its control over the Council's decisions" (*Clarín* 1996a, 2–3). By June 1996 it appeared that the chamber would stymie Menem's initiative.[28]

In response, Menem threatened to begin using decree powers to name judges (Boschi 1996, 6). At that time, vacancies existed in twenty-one federal judicial posts. However, these positions could not be filled because the new constitution stipulated that only the council could select candidates for judgeships after the termination of the one-year interim period. With Menem content not to face council-appointed judges, the government decided to "freeze" debate on the council for the time being.

Menem briefly became interested in the council, due to pressures from the International Monetary Fund (IMF), the following summer. On July 15, 1997, Menem called a meeting with his new minister of justice and the head of the Senate's Constitutional Affairs Commission. Menem informed them that "the Minister of the Economy, Roque Fernandez, [was] in New York negotiating a loan with the IMF, and IMF officials had, once again, expressed their preoccupation with the Argentine judiciary's lack of independence, its inefficiency, and the long delay in the creation of the Council. [The minister of justice] told the president that he had received similar comments from the international organization" (Ventura 1998a, 268). But although the president may have felt the need to give lip service to the IMF about the council, he was not concerned enough about pressures from the IMF to actually establish it. And though Menem procrastinated, the IMF did not penalize Argentina for its lack of progress on the council's creation.

With respect to economic pressures for judicial reform, the Argentine government was also well aware of the wisdom linking a successful private sector–led economy with an independent and efficient judiciary. According to Humberto Quiroga Lavie, ideas connecting a well-functioning judiciary to economic growth had been circulating in Argentina since the early 1990s (Quiroga Lavie 1999).[29] Several studies by prominent Argentine think tanks in the early 1990s had indicated that judicial delays and incompetence had serious repercussions for the costs of doing business in their country.[30] Indeed, Menem's economic minister, Domingo Cavallo, gave a speech in 1992 on the need to improve Argentina's "judicial security" in order to foster the country's economic growth.[31] But although Argentine leaders were well aware of the relationship between judicial independence and economic performance, the ruling party remained content to delay progress on the council.

The president's interest in a council, however, began to change when the next round of congressional elections dramatically altered the political landscape. The Peronists were resoundingly defeated by "the Alliance," a center-left coalition uniting the Radicals and Frepaso (Frente Pais Solidario, Country Solidarity Front),[32] in the October 1997 midterm elections. Nationally, the Peronists garnered only 36.2 percent of the vote, compared with 45.7 percent for the Alliance (*Clarín* 1997c). In the city of Buenos Aires, the vote was overwhelmingly in favor of the Alliance over the Peronists, 56.7 to 17.98 percent (*Clarín* 1997c). The Peronists suffered a major upset in the state of Buenos Aires, which they had expected to win, losing 48 to 41.3 percent (*Latin American Regional Report* 1997, 6). They were also defeated in the states of Santa Fe and Entre Rios, two traditional Peronist strongholds. In addition, the Alliance took control of the Chamber of Deputies.

With the 1997 midterm election, it became clear that the Peronists' chances of winning the presidential election in 1999 were fading. The 1997 election was expected "to define in good measure the terrain for the presidential race in 1999" (*Clarín* 1997a). This had been true of the 1987 congressional election, in which the rout of the Radicals had been taken as a strong predictor of their defeat in the 1989 presidential election. In fact, "the [Peronist] government's reverse [was] more drastic than that suffered by the Radicals in 1987" and "gave the impression of a hard blow" against the Peronists' 1999 presidential prospects (*Clarín* 1997b).

As for the strong performance of the Alliance in the 1997 election, judicial concerns had been one of its campaign's top priorities. The Radical-Frepaso coalition had called for the immediate establishment of the

Judicial Council and had also demanded changes in the membership of the court (*La Nación* 1997b, 8). An Alliance proposal for an independent council was passed in the Chamber immediately after the new legislature took office. It proposed the creation of a twenty-member council with representatives from all three branches of government, the majority and minority political parties, and legal professionals. The mixed membership guaranteed that no single party or political group could control it. Furthermore, the council was granted all the responsibilities originally assigned to it in the 1994 constitution. The bill was sent to the Senate, where it was signed into law on December 18, 1997.[33]

It must be remembered that Menem still controlled the Senate at that time, and the president could have blocked the bill's passage. Yet he allowed the Alliance's proposal to be passed in the upper house, thereby acceding to the creation of an independent judicial council. According to council member Quiroga Lavie, eleven of the members were independent and nine had ties to the government (Quiroga Lavie 1999). However, by delaying the selection of council members, Menem postponed the establishment of the council for more than a year. In fact, the council's representatives were not sworn in until November 18, 1998,[34] and the council only began operating in early 1999—nearly five years after the promulgation of Argentina's new constitution. Yet because it would take at least six months for the council to name judges, the earliest that council-appointed judges would be on the bench was not until the end of 1999—at a time when it was extremely unlikely that Menem would still be in office.[35] By November 1998 the Alliance was polling 40.3 percent versus the Peronists' 27.6 percent for the next presidential election.[36] Thus, the council that Menem had agreed to establish in 1994 would finally serve to check presidential power, but the true costs of the council were to be passed on to Argentina's next president.[37]

Analyzing Argentina's Judicial Reform:
Initiation and Delayed Implementation

In 1994, with the initiation of judicial reform, Menem appeared willing to cede his control of the court, to decrease the partisanship of future Supreme Court justices, and to establish a judicial council to strengthen the independence of the judicial branch. In exchange for these constitutional judicial changes, the Peronists received specific and immediate benefits. First, agreeing to Radical demands to free the judiciary from executive influence was the only way in which Menem could obtain the right to a consecutive re-election. The Radicals had made this explicitly clear in both their private and public statements about constitutional reform.

Second, writing a judicial council into the constitution satisfied international financial institutions, which benefited the Peronists' ability to access foreign funding. It also satisfied the Radical Party who was seeking to decrease the ability of the executive to intervene in the judicial branch. The *Acuerdo de Olivos*, though it did include a general agreement to decrease politicization of the judiciary, makes no mention of a judicial council.[38] In fact, neither the Radicals nor the Peronists had ever suggested the creation of a judicial council in any of their previous individual proposals or bipartisan pacts. Instead, the idea of a council emerged as a result of the involvement of international organizations in Argentina's judicial reform. According to Alberto García-Lema, a chief member of Menem's negotiating team, the Radical-Peronist constitutional commission responsible for proposing judicial reform relied heavily on the International Development Bank's September 1993 *Report on the Reform of the Administration of Justice in Argentina*, a document that advocated the creation of a council to promote judicial independence and to modernize court administration.[39] From the viewpoint of the Peronists, they had already agreed in principle to increase judicial independence. With a judicial council, they could simultaneously satisfy international financial institutions, which could provide access to economic assistance, and the Radicals, who were needed to approve constitutional reforms.

Thus, the initiation of judicial reform had direct benefits for Menem and his party. And, while it also had potential costs, these were minimized because they could be evaded or postponed. First, Menem did not force the third justice to resign in February 1994. When the justice finally stepped down, the Peronists rapidly filled his position, in a move of dubious legality, with a Menemista justice. Second, although the Peronists had agreed to increasing confirmation of prospective justices (to two-thirds of the Senate), the cost of this pledge was minimized because it was uncertain if a vacancy on the court would occur during Menem's second term. Finally, as for the council, the costs of this new institution would be imposed only upon passage of congressional legislation. Given the high likelihood that Menem would return to office and that his party would control at least one congressional branch in 1995, the details of this legislation, and vigor with which it would be sought, would most likely remain at the Peronists' discretion.

With respect to the Radicals, the initiation of judicial reform also had benefits. According to Argentine political scientist Catalina Smulovitz, Alfonsín believed that if immediate re-election was not possible, a stand-in for Menem would most likely win the 1995 presidential election, and that the highly popular Menem would then run again for the presidency in 2001. Thus, from the point of view of Alfonsín, the most likely scenario was twelve more years of Menemista government. Faced with the strong possibility of the Peronists in power until 2007, Alfonsín opted instead to enable Menem to run again, but to hold office for only four more years, and thereby allow the Radicals a better chance of winning back the presidency in 1999 (as indeed they did) (Smulovitz 1999).[40] In addition, opinion polls at that time indicated that 70 percent of the population favored a national constitutional assembly to allow re-election, making it difficult for the Radicals to oppose a constitutional convention.

With the Acuerdo, the Radicals believed they were obtaining judicial checks on executive power. First, they believed that a Radical-dominated Supreme Court would be an effective constraint on the re-elected president. They also received other institutional judicial advancements. For example, should a member of the new Radical-majority court resign, the two-thirds Senate confirmation meant that Menem could not name a partisan appointee. In addition, the Radicals believed they were removing executive influence over lower-level judges via the creation of the Council.[41] Furthermore, the Radicals also believed that they were receiving several additional institutional reforms that would augment their ability to constrain the re-elected president, including the direct election of the mayor of Buenos Aires (which they expected to win) and additional seats in the Senate (which would allow them to break Menem's two-thirds domination).

Clearly, for the Radicals the initiation of judicial reform was not without its costs; Menem obtained the right to re-election. However, the real costs did not become apparent until the court was not delivered to them, but by then it was too late to alter course. The third justice, who had announced his February 1994 resignation, was still on the court when the constitutional convention opened in May 1994. Yet for several reasons the Radicals proceeded to uphold their end of the deal: first, because of the public's overwhelming support for constitutional reform; second, because reneging on the deal would have made it appear that the Radicals were only interested in control over the court; and third, because the new constitution's other institutional changes improved the Radicals' political position.

Thus, for both the Peronists and the Radicals, the benefits of the initiation of judicial reform outweighed its costs, and both parties could agree to proceed with constitutional revisions. However, once Menem was re-elected, his cost/benefit analysis of judicial reform changed dramatically. Although he would obtain no additional political benefit from relinquishing his hold over the court or from setting up an independent judicial council (the Radicals had nothing new to offer and the IFIs were not linking economic assistance to the creation of such a council), real implementation of his bargain would impose great costs: the establishment of real judicial constraints on executive authority. Thus, with his re-election, Menem had no incentive to proceed with implementation and accept the costs of judicial reform. In contrast, the Radicals, who sought the legislative enactment of judicial reform, did not possess the political power necessary to implement it.

In the end Menem never altered the membership of Argentina's Supreme Court. A court allied with the president served Menem's interests: it prevented judicial constraints upon his authority during his administration and could also protect him and his established policies in the future. On the other hand, Menem did eventually allow the establishment of an independent judicial council. Menem could have blocked passage of the council via his control of the Senate but did not. It was neither the demands of the Radicals nor the concerns of the IFIs that proved sufficient to entice the president to create the council. Rather, its creation coincided with the dramatic deterioration of the government's political position in October 1997, a reversal that signaled the likely defeat of the Peronists in 1999. Once Menem perceived that his party would not retain office, he had the incentive to seek the establishment of the council, albeit one that would become effective only after his presidential term had expired.

In conclusion, judicial reform in Argentina in the 1990s was a case of initiation of constitutional increases in judicial power followed by their delayed enactment. In 1994 the ruling party was apparently willing to decrease its influence over the Supreme Court and to strengthen the independence of the national judiciary via the creation of a judicial council. In exchange for these judicial changes, the ruling party received specific benefits. First, these changes satisfied the international financial institutions. Second, and more importantly, agreeing to increases in judicial independence was the only way the president could obtain the right to reelection. However, neither of these two benefits was sufficient to induce the ruling party to follow through with reform and accept the costs of real judicial independence. In the end, Menem never gave up his control over the court. However, in December 1997, once it appeared that the Peronists' political power was evaporating, he allowed passage of legislation to establish an independent judicial council. While Menem never confronted the costs of two-thirds Senate approval of prospective justices or of council-appointed judges, these changes bode well for the development of a judiciary free from executive interference in Argentina.

Chapter Three

Judicial Reform in Peru in the 1990s

After twelve years of military rule, Peru returned to democracy in 1980 with free and fair elections. For the next ten years, the country was governed by the two traditional parties but neither proved capable of solving the problems of double-digit inflation, economic crisis, or internal terrorism that beset the country. Alberto Fujimori, a university dean and political outsider who had never previously held office, came to power in the 1990 presidential election. Two years later, on April 5, 1992, President Fujimori's military-backed *"auto-golpe"* (self-coup) closed Peru's Congress, fired the country's Supreme Court and Constitutional Court justices, and centralized all power in the executive's hands. While the coup was applauded by Peru's population at home, the international community protested Fujimori's suspension of constitutional rule. Given intense international pressure, Fujimori announced that the country would return to democratic rule following the convocation of a national assembly to rewrite Peru's constitution.

Peru's new constitution, effective January 1, 1994, enhanced executive power and allowed for immediate presidential re-election. Yet at the same time, it also increased the independence and authority of the judicial branch. Specifically, the 1993 constitution introduced institutional changes that appeared to greatly empower the country's judicial branch, including the creation of a powerful judicial council and a reinvigorated constitutional court. However, following Fujimori's 1995 re-election the president failed to follow through with the meaningful implementation of the judicial advancements to which he had previously agreed. Instead, he used his political power to systematically destroy all judicial autonomy. In 1996

Peru's judicial branch was placed under an executive committee; shortly thereafter, both the Judicial Council and Constitutional Court ceased functioning as a result of executive actions. Only after Fujimori was forced to resign, following a September 2000 corruption scandal, did the president reverse his relentless onslaught against the judiciary and revoke executive control over the judicial branch.

The first section of this chapter discusses the traditional Peruvian judiciary and Fujimori's contentious relationship with the judicial branch during his first two years in office. The second section outlines the institutional reforms to the judiciary codified at Peru's 1992–93 constitutional convention. The following section details Fujimori's attack on the judiciary between 1994 and 2000. The next section demonstrates the rapid reversal of his judicial strategy with his meteoric fall from power in 2000. The last section applies my argument to Peru to explain that country's experience with judicial reform. In Peru, as in Argentina in the 1990s, while the president could be induced to *initiate* reforms, he then proved unwilling to accept judicial constraints and therefore failed to follow through with the *implementation* of these constitutional changes. Only once the president saw his political fortunes plummet did he dismantle executive domination of the judicial branch.

The Judiciary Prior to the 1993 Constitution

Peru's Traditional Judiciary

"The judiciary in Peru, as in many other Latin American nations, has historically been the weakest branch of government, by design and by abandon" (Comisión de Juristas Internacionales 1994, 31). Peru's earliest constitutions established the judiciary as an independent branch of government, but "one enters the judiciary fundamentally due to political favors" (De Belaunde 1991, 27), and the judiciary in Peru has "always been tied to political power" (García Belaunde n.d., 67). While the Peruvian judiciary had been subject to a myriad of reforms throughout the nineteenth and twentieth centuries, none of these had enabled the courts to develop as a check on political power.

Peru's 1979 constitution, written in a multiparty constitutional convention as part of the return to civilian rule, attempted to address the traditional weakness of the country's judicial branch. First, the 1979 constitution created a national magistrates council (called a national judicial council in most other Latin American countries) to propose candidates to fill judicial posts. These included justices of the Supreme Court, first- and second-level judges, as well as the posts known as *fiscales*. (*Fiscales* are prosecutors responsible for investigating allegations of state wrongdoing.)[1] However, a fundamental weakness plaguing the council was that the Peruvian president was not bound to appoint an individual from the council's list of nominees (Comisión de Juristas Internacionales 1994, 79). Crippled by its inability to enforce executive compliance, the National Magistrates Council was therefore unable to foster real independence within the judicial branch. In fact, politicization of the judiciary became even more pronounced after the return to democracy in 1979 than it had been in the past. According to Peruvian legal expert Linn Hammergren, "Party identification emerged in the 1980s as a primary factor in naming and promoting judges. To an extent never seen before, judges were identified as sympathizers with one or another party . . . party identification or personal connections had always influenced appointments. They now were often the only criteria" (Hammergren 1998a, 149–50).

A second fundamental innovation of Peru's 1979 constitution was the establishment of a constitutional court with the power of judicial review. In other words, the Constitutional Court, unlike the Supreme Court, is authorized to declare laws found unconstitutional as *null and void for all citizens*. (While the Peruvian Supreme Court may declare a law "unconstitutional" in its application to the individual who brought the suit, the law itself remains in effect for the rest of the citizenry.) However, Peru's Constitutional Court remained ineffectual in the 1980s because its naming process had left it tied to the presidency in the period immediately following the return to democratic rule.[2]

The 1979 constitution intended to promote the judiciary's ability to serve as a check upon the other branches of government, but the results were clearly less than satisfactory. Institutional flaws, such as executive influence and the degree of politicization in the judiciary, contributed to the low status of the judicial branch. Additional internal factors, in particular the rampant corruption pervading the entire judicial branch and the institution's poor quality of service, cemented the judiciary's negative image in the eyes of the public (De Belaunde 1991).[3] From Fujimori's first day in office, the president attacked the judiciary. Many saw this as an astute public relations maneuver that was well received by the general public (Rospigliosi 1997). Others, at least in hindsight, saw Fujimori's early criticism of the judiciary as part of a larger campaign to excoriate all of Peru's traditional political institutions, thereby setting the stage for his 1992 "self-coup."

Fujimori's Contentious Relationship with the Judicial Branch, 1990–1992

Fujimori's confrontational relationship with the judiciary began with his inaugural address, in which he referred to Peru's Supreme Court as the "Palace of Injustice" (Abad Yupanqui and Garcés Peralta 1993, 99). The following month the president again harshly criticized the judiciary but this time specifically cited its level of corruption.[4] Fujimori's relationship with the judiciary became more acerbic during the next two years, as the president continued to publicly denigrate the judicial branch, on the one hand, and as the two high courts proved willing to rule against the president's key interests, on the other.

First, with respect to the Supreme Court, Fujimori wanted the court to try Peru's former president, Alan García, for illicit enrichment while in office. The justices on the Supreme Court, many of whom had been appointed by Garcia, refused to open a case against him. Fujimori's response was to impose Decree Law 767 (December 1991), thereby adding seven justices to Peru's twenty-three-member Supreme Court.[5] However, with the Supreme Court's March 1992 decision to release from custody the suspected head of the terrorist group Shining Path[6]—a decision counter to Fujimori's antiterrorism campaign—it became clear that the court packing had failed to obtain the degree of influence over the court that the president had been seeking. Fujimori then attempted to impeach several members of the Supreme Court, but the ploy became moot when all of Peru's Supreme Court justices were fired in his *auto-golpe* the following month.

While the Supreme Court hampered the success of Fujimori's antiterrorist campaign, Peru's Constitutional Court threatened the implementation of the president's economic program. Between 1990 and 1992 the Court declared nine laws to be unconstitutional, ruling against Fujimori more times in two years than it had against the two previous presidents combined (Abad Yupanqui 1995). Three of these rulings occurred in February and March 1992, in the weeks just prior to Fujimori's coup. In February the court ruled unconstitutional an executive decree limiting benefits owed to retirees. In the same month, the court also found unconstitutional a decree liberalizing the price of public urban transport.[7] In March the Constitutional Court declared partially unconstitutional a decree law intended to promote private investment in state-owned enterprises. At that time supporters of Fujimori's economic program "feared that if the Constitutional Court declared the unconstitutionality of the decree in its entirety, the government would remain completely impeded from achieving its role in economic matters" (Abad Yupanqui and Garcés Peralta 1993, 140). Thus, by early 1992 both of Peru's high courts had demonstrated their power to challenge the government.

The Initiation of Judicial Reform in Peru:
The *Fujigolpe* and Peru's 1992–1993 Constitutional Convention

On April 5, 1992, Fujimori's executive-led *auto-golpe* suspended the entire government apparatus, fired all justices and judges in the country, and declared the country to be in a period of "national reorganization." Fujimori had cultivated relations with the Peruvian military—in particular relying on one of his chief advisers, Vladimir Montesinos, a shadowy figure who served as the liaison between Fujimori and the military—and the *golpe* was backed by Peru's armed forces (Schmidt 2000; Mauceri 1995).[8] Peru's citizenry, convinced that Peru's traditional political institutions impeded the resolution of the country's economic and social ills, overwhelmingly supported the *golpe*.[9] The international community, however, strongly criticized Fujimori's actions. In a press statement on April 6, the Organization of American States (OAS) demanded an immediate return to democratic rule. Both the United States and the European Community suspended all funds to Peru (except humanitarian aid), and the Inter-American Development Bank suspended over $200 million in loans and grants (Abad Yupanqui and Garcés Peralta 1993, 157). With an eye toward renewing access to international funding, Fujimori announced Peru's impending return to democratic government following the convocation of a national assembly to rewrite the country's constitution.

Representatives to the Democratic Constitutional Convention, or CCD, were chosen in a national election in late October and took their seats in December 1992. Fujimori had a majority in the CCD and controlled its Constitutional Commission, the committee responsible for determining the version of the constitution that would be voted on by the convention. Interestingly, unlike many constitutional conventions, which required a supermajority of delegates to approve constitutional revisions, Peru's 1992–93 convention required only a simple majority to approve constitutional changes. Since Fujimori controlled both the commission and the CCD, he was easily able to design the new constitution. However, Peru's rewritten constitution also needed to be ratified by the public in a national referendum before it could be promulgated. Thus, although the president did not confront in the CCD an opposition that could force him to modify his reform proposals, he did confront a source of "opposition" with which he would have to bargain.

In fact, with respect to the judiciary, the final version of the constitution submitted to the public for ratification differed tremendously from the government's first proposal. The Constitutional Commission initially solicited judicial reform proposals from respected members of the academic and legal community, and the forthcoming proposals strengthened the judicial branch (García Belaunde 1997). But rather than accept any of these proposals, the Fujimori-controlled commission wrote up its own proposal, which abolished the Constitutional Court and allowed the executive and legislative branches to have ultimate authority over judicial selection (García Belaunde 1997). Thus, the government originally sought to weaken the judiciary and maintain a high degree of influence over it.

However, opinion polls in late June 1993 demonstrated that public support for the revised constitution was waning and that the population particularly opposed the elimination of the Constitutional Court (*Caretas* 1993, 16).[10] According to Domingo García Belaunde, an opposition member at the constitutional convention, "Surveys conducted by the National Intelligence Service showed that the constitution would not pass in the referendum, in particular because the public was concerned with the lack of judicial guarantees. So, at the last minute, the government reintroduced 70% of the reforms [judicial advancements drafted by opposition members at the constitutional convention] we originally proposed" (García Belaunde 1997). Thus, the Constitutional Commission reintroduced the Constitutional Court and granted the National Magistrates Council complete control over the naming and discipline of judges and fiscales, two changes the government identified as necessary for obtaining public approval. In the national referendum held on October 31, 1993, the Peruvian electorate ratified the new constitution 52 percent to 48 percent (García Belaunde 1996, 390).

Peru's resulting 1993 constitution increased both presidential power and judicial independence. With respect to the former, the new constitution granted the president the right to re-election. It also broadened the range of presidential decree powers and strengthened the presidency vis-à-vis the Congress. By reducing Peru's traditional two-chamber body to a unicameral legislature, the new constitution facilitated the president's ability to enact laws. In addition, the president was granted the right to dissolve Congress once during his presidential tenure.

At the same time, the new constitution granted increased independence to the judicial branch. The new National Magistrates Council, a strengthened version of the 1979 constitution's council, was given complete control over the naming of all judges and *fiscales* in Peru. Specifically, the council was to fill judicial and fiscales posts via performance on national examinations, thus all magistrate positions would now be merit based. The council would have the power to appoint justices to the Supreme Court and fiscales to the Supreme Junta without any executive intervention, making it one of the most powerful judicial councils in the world. The council was also given disciplinary power over all magistrates, including the power to sanction, suspend, or remove judges and fiscales. Finally, the council would "ratify" all magistrates every seven years, with renewal in office dependent on a clean performance record. The council's membership, explicitly defined in the constitution, guaranteed that it could not be controlled by either of the other two branches of government.

The 1993 constitution also re-established Peru's Constitutional Court. In the past, the president, the Congress, and the Supreme Court each appointed three members for a total of nine justices. The new constitution reduced the number of members on the Constitutional Court by two and altered their selection process. Now, the seven-member court would be chosen by Congress, with the approval of two-thirds of the congressional membership. This would most likely force the ruling party to choose more moderate candidates in a compromise with opposition parties in Congress.

In addition, the new constitution included several other positive changes that appeared to promote the development of the judicial branch.[11] It created a judicial academy to prepare judges and fiscales for merit-examinations administered by the council. The academy was charged with establishing a judicial curriculum for university students, designing training programs, and administering additional courses of study for magistrates seeking promotions. The 1993 constitution also affirmed the existing "justices of the peace," trained individuals who provide judicial resolution of conflicts in areas traditionally lacking access to the regular court system.[12]

On balance, the new constitution both strengthened the power of the executive and increased the judiciary's potential to check that power.[13] The first president of the new National Magistrates Council stated that he was pleased with the 1993 constitution's apparent increases in judicial independence and with the powers of the reformed council (Montoya Anguerry 1997). The United States–Peru Bilateral Commission, established to analyze Peru's 1993 constitution, reported, "The new Constitution can contribute to the depoliticization of a process that has been corrupted for years in Peru and so may well mark the first step directed at the creation of a genuine and independent judiciary" (Comisión de Juristas Internacionales 1994, 111). According to Linn Hammergren, "The constitution significantly reduced the formal ability of the other branches of government to interfere with judicial and prosecutorial independence" (Hammergren 1998a, 179). Thus, the initiation of judicial reform was successfully achieved in Peru in 1993. To convert these new constitutional principles into law, however, required the passage of implementing legislation in Congress.

The Implementation of Judicial Reform Under Fujimori:
Erosion of Judicial Independence, 1995–2000

The following sections detail the evisceration of judicial independence during implementation, first by Peru's temporary Congress in 1994–95 and then by the 1995–2000 Congress.

The Implementation of Judicial Reforms Under Peru's Temporary Congress

From the 1992 coup throughout the period of the constitutional convention, Fujimori ruled by decree. Peru's new constitution took effect January 1, 1994, but new elections were not scheduled until July 1995. During the interim between January 1994 and July 1995, Fujimori continued to wield a great deal of influence over the two other branches of government. First, the Fujimori-dominated CCD served as the country's "temporary Congress," thereby leaving the president in control of the legislature. Second, all judicial posts in the country, after having been vacated with the coup's mass firing of magistrates, had been renamed with "provisional" Fujimori-appointees.[14] The "provisional" status of magistrates "signifie[d] that they can be terminated or transferred at any moment without any reason. The absence of guaranteed judicial stability makes judges submissive and can compromise their independence and objectivity" (Comisión de Juristas Internacionales 1994, 106). In late 1992 Fujimori established the Tribunal of Honor to review petitions from ceased magistrates with respect to their reinstatement and to "tenure" (grant permanence to) the provisional magistrates he had named.[15] In early 1994, the tribunal tenured the justices on the Supreme Court and the fiscales on the Supreme Junta, but only a handful of superior-level judges and *fiscales* were officially ratified.[16] Almost all first- and second-level magistrates remained provisional.

Peru's temporary Congress was responsible for enacting the legislation required to convert the constitution's newly enshrined judicial institutions into a working reality. The Organic Law of the Judiciary, passed in October 1994, officially established the National Magistrates Council and the Judicial Academy. The council's members took their posts in

March 1995, eager to begin tenuring magistrates. However, the council could tenure magistrates only once they passed a council-administered examination— and magistrates could sit for this examination only after completing a preparatory course at the Judicial Academy. The government delayed the staffing of the Judicial Academy, thereby preventing it from offering courses. By employing this stratagem, Fujimori effectively delayed the operation of the council and, hence, the naming of tenured, and potentially independent, magistrates.

Peru's temporary Congress also enacted the legislation defining the country's Constitutional Court (the Organic Law of the Constitutional Court) in January 1995. First, the Organic Law stipulated that a supermajority (six out of seven) of justices would be required in order for the Constitutional Court to declare laws or acts unconstitutional.[17] In consequence, laws found to be unconstitutional by even five of the seven justices would remain in effect, greatly eroding the power of the court to check government authority. In addition, the government delayed the naming of its justices, thereby postponing the date at which the administration would have to contend with the court. Hence, the temporary Congress both delayed the Constitutional Court's establishment and undermined its powers.

Implementation After Fujimori's 1995 Re-election:
The National Magistrates Council and the Judicial Academy

In July 1995 Peru returned to democratic rule with national elections. Fujimori easily recaptured the presidency and was awarded a majority in the now unicameral legislature (67 of 120 seats).[18] Immediately following its inauguration in November 1995, Peru's new Congress passed a "judicial reform" law; this was the first of many "surprise" laws affecting the judiciary which would be passed during Fujimori's second administration. This law, Law 26546, set up an executive commission, presided over by the Supreme Court chief justice, to govern the judicial branch for the next year. The chief justice, counter to all intuition, then delegated his powers to Fujimori's hand-picked member of the commission, José Dellepiane. In other words, the Supreme Court chief justice willfully relinquished control of the judiciary to the executive branch.[19]

Thus, as of November 1995, an executive commission was overseeing the Peruvian judiciary while all other judicial institutions—the National Magistrates Council, the Judicial Academy, and the Constitutional Court—remained inoperational. In addition, the country's judiciary remained characterized by the "untenured" status of its magistrates. More than 1,300 judges and *fiscales* named by Fujimori during the suspension of constitutional rule remained provisional (Montoya Anguerry 2001). In order to tenure these provisional magistrates, the council decided to "assume" the responsibility of administering training courses (Montoya Anguerry 2001). The council trained magistrates and conducted examinations in the first half of 1996 and proceeded to name two supreme fiscales and 151 superior-level judges and fiscales.

In June 1996, five months before the Executive Commission was to expire, the government passed its next major judicial reform law, Law 26623.[20] On the surface, this law appeared to return control over the judiciary to the judicial branch. It created a new governing body for the judicial branch (the Judicial Coordinating Council), with the body's membership drawn from various judicial and legal institutions. However, the real effect of Law 26623 was revealed in the law's transitory provisions (*transitorios*). The first provision stated that this new governing body would remain "suspended" until December 31, 1998. Until that time, the judiciary would remain under the control of the existing Executive Commission, and the chief justice redesignated Dellepiane as the commission's president. Thus, the real intent of Law 26623 was to extend Fujimori's control over the judicial branch for the next two and a half years.[21]

Law 26623's long list of additional transitory provisions continued to chip away at the judiciary's autonomy. One *transitorio* declared the Judicial Academy to be under "reorganization" and officially placed it under the Executive Commission.[22] In addition, the Judicial Academy would now evaluate not only judges' knowledge of the law but also their "moral correctness," and the academy was granted the ability to "separate" judges from their posts. Technically, the Magistrates Council was the only institution constitutionally empowered to suspend, terminate, or in any way "separate" judges.

Another of Law 26623's *transitorios* guaranteed that the position of Supreme Court chief justice would be a "Fujimorista." The post of chief justice is a powerful one because it determines the assignment of justices to specific chambers (for example, the constitutional law chamber or the penal chamber) of the court. These chambers, composed of four or five members, may rule on cases without the involvement of other justices. In the past, members of the Supreme Court had elected the chief justice for a one-year period. Now, as a result of Law 26623, the Supreme Court's "Vocal Decano" would serve as the Court's chief justice. "Vocal Decano" is the title given to the oldest justice on the court (as measured by date of birth and not years served). Thus, the chief justice would now permanently be Victor Castillo Castillo, the oldest member of the court and a known "Fujimorista" (Cubas 1997b). By guaranteeing ownership of the position of chief justice, Fujimori ensured that "amenable" justices controlled the politically important chambers.

Finally, another transitory provision of Law 26623 gave the Executive Commission the power of "legal initiative" within the judiciary. This allowed the commission to issue administrative resolutions to continuously manipulate the judiciary to suit the government's interests.[23] After Law 26623, "then began the daily changes, you had to read the new judicial laws every day" to discover what changes had been dictated overnight (Ugaz 1997). Regardless of its earlier constitutional promises of 1993, with the passage of Law 26623 it became clear that the government had no intention of allowing the judicial branch to develop as a check on the exercise of government power.[24]

In the month following the enactment of Law 26623, July 1996, the National Magistrates Council conducted a round of examinations to fill positions for second-instance judges and *fiscales*. The government, worried about the possibility of tenured magistrates' demonstrating independence, opted to use its control over the Judicial Academy (now under the Executive Commission) to extend the duration of judicial training courses and thereby prevent the council from holding examinations to tenure more judges and *fiscales*.[25] In August the National Magistrates Council issued a press statement in which it expressed concern for the impartiality and independence of judges. In December 1996 the council concluded its third round of examinations.[26] One week later, the Peruvian Congress passed Law 26696, which suspended the council's ability to conduct examinations. Thus, no more magistrates would be granted tenure, and Peru's more than one thousand unratified judges and *fiscales* would remain "provisional." A second December 1996 law suspended the constitutional requirement that superior-level *fiscales* possess a minimum of ten years of experience before being promoted to the position of supreme fiscal.[27] This was designed to facilitate the government's ability to place more malleable individuals on the Supreme Junta of Fiscales (Cubas 1997b).

Fujimori's political manipulation of the judiciary continued in early 1997 as the Executive Commission granted itself the right to create and disband courts at will, to assign judges to particular courts, and to appoint provisional judges and *fiscales*, including provisional Supreme Court justices and Supreme Junta *fiscales*. The commission recognized that it could not fire the "tenured" judges that existed; thus, as an alternative, it began to transfer them out of politically important judgeships. In this way, the commission replaced independent judges in key posts with sympathetic, provisional magistrates. Because justices and *fiscales* at the supreme level could not be assigned to another court or junta (magistrates could be transferred only to a position of equal rank), the commission packed both institutions with provisional members.[28]

Two examples of the Executive Commission's use of its new powers include the disbanding of the Anti-Drug Court and the replacement of tenured judges by provisional ones on Lima's Superior Public Law Court. With respect to the former, Peru's Anti-Drug Court was established on February 12, 1997, supposedly as part of the government's strategy to eradicate illegal drug trafficking. Dr. Ines Villa Bonilla, the court's presiding judge, quickly moved to subpoena several top members of the military, including the president's chief adviser, Vladimir Montesinos. Two weeks later, on February 27, 1997, the Executive Commission abruptly disbanded the court. The commission announced that all drug-trafficking cases would now be heard by the Supreme Court's recently created "Second Temporary Penal Chamber." Not only were all five justices assigned to that chamber provisional, but the chamber's presiding justice, Alejandro Rodriguez Medrano, was a known bribe taker and a "friend" of the National Intelligence Service (Cubas 1997b). As expected, the Temporary Penal Chamber failed to pursue any other allegation of narcotrafficking committed by the military or other influential supporters of the president.

A second example of the commission's 1997 machinations involved Lima's Superior Public Law Court. The three tenured judges on that court, each of whom had ruled against the military in several cases of human rights violations, were replaced with provisional judges (*Portada* 1997, 6–8). In fact, the court's respected presiding judge, Sergio Salas, was replaced by Sixto Muñoz Saramiento, a judge who had been sanctioned for judicial misconduct in the past. With its judicial interventions, the government was now actively seeking not only to prevent judicial challenges to its authority, but also to use the courts to protect its allies and to intimidate its opponents.

Despite all its scheming, the government was still not satisfied with its control of the judiciary, as evidenced by the August 1997 comments of Carlos Torres, speaker of Peru's Congress: "The judiciary still needs a major reform."[29] In particular, the government began emphasizing the need to engage in "jurisdictional" judicial reform, although what was meant by the government's new catch phrase was never made clear. Regardless of the "type" of the reform, the effect of these continuous interventions in the judiciary was a decrease in the already incredibly low status of the judicial branch. Public opinion polls taken at the time of Torres's declaration showed that 64 percent of the population believed the judiciary to be more dependent on the government than it was in the past,[30] and that seven out of ten Peruvians disapproved of the judicial branch.[31]

The government's assault on the judiciary started anew with the passage in December 1997 of Law 26898, a law designed to increase the power of Peru's provisional magistrates. Traditionally, Peru's tenured Supreme Court justices and Supreme Junta *fiscales* in Peru enjoyed certain privileges that were not shared with their provisional-status colleagues. Specifically, only tenured Supreme-level magistrates could serve as representatives of their institution on another government body or vote on decisions taken by their respective institutions. Law 26898 declared that all provisional Supreme-level justices and *fiscales* were now "equalized," meaning they would enjoy the rights previously reserved for tenured magistrates. While the details are complicated, the true political ramification of Law 26898 was to ensure Fujimori's right to run for a third—and illegal—presidential term by packing the body that was to determine the legality of another consecutive term (Cubas 1997a).[32] Congressmen from opposition parties, the National Magistrates Council, and legal scholars outspokenly criticized the change in voting status effected by Law 26898, but to no avail.[33]

Fujimori's final blow to the judicial branch occurred three months later when Congress passed Law 26933 and effectively eliminated the last of the National Magistrates Council's power. The March 1998 law stated that the Executive Commission would now be responsible for investigating allegations of corruption in its institution and for determining appropriate sanctions for those found guilty of misconduct.[34] A week before the law was announced, the National Magistrates Council had initiated an investigation of six Supreme Court justices for allegedly accepting a bribe to alter their ruling in a case. As a result of Law 26933, the investigation was removed from the council's jurisdiction and placed under the Executive Commission, with no further action taken (Rodríguez Iturri 1998, 7).

Thus, by March 1998 all of the Magistrates Council's constitutionally granted powers, including the right to examine, to name, to investigate, to discipline, and to fire magistrates, had each been eliminated or usurped by the Executive Commission. In response to Law 26933, the council's membership resigned *en masse,* and the council was replaced with a more compliant membership (Montoya Anguerry 1998). As for the academy at this time, with nearly three hundred provisional magistrates nearing the completion of their judicial preparatory course, the academy announced that these magistrates would be named as *suplentes* ("supplementals"— meaning without tenure protection) rather than as tenured judges and *fiscales* (Rubio 1998).

On November 22, 1998, the head of the Executive Commission, David Pezua (who had replaced Dellepiane in the fall of 1998 when it appeared that Dellepiane was no longer willing to follow the government's lead), asked for a two-year extension of the commission because Peru's judicial reform was "only 60% complete" (*El Comercio* 1998a, A4). (Interestingly, twelve days earlier Pezua had requested only a one-year extension; *La Republica* 1998, 9.) In early December 1998, with the Executive Commission set to expire at the end of the month, Peru's Congress passed a law to extend the commission's duration for another two years. In other words, the executive branch would continue to control the judiciary until December 2000, thereby guaranteeing Fujimori's ability to manipulate the council and the academy to suit his political interests throughout the rest of his second term in office.

Implementation After Fujimori's 1995 Re-election:
Erosion of the Constitutional Court

The government's strategy with respect to the implementation of the Constitutional Court, paralleling that of its strategy toward the judicial branch, was to delay the court's commencement of operations and to undermine its powers. With regard to the former, the government opted to prevent the naming of the court's justices. Peru's 1993 constitution stipulated that two-thirds of the members of Congress were required to approve Constitutional Court nominees. But because the government controlled only a congressional majority, it could not unilaterally appoint nominees. Consequently, the administration proposed candidates who, because of their strong ties to the government or military, were completely unacceptable to the opposition and thereby postponed the date at which the court would sit. Finally, a year and a half later, in June 1996 the government and the opposition compromised on a slate of appointees. Of these, two justices were considered to be in the government's pocket (Jimenez 1998). Thus, given the stipulation passed by the temporary Congress requiring six of the seven justices to rule a law unconstitutional, it was unlikely that the court could effectively block the Fujimori administration.[35]

With the membership of the Constitutional Court officially chosen, the government then proceeded to pass two additional amendments to Peru's Organic Law of the Constitutional Court. The first established that the court be located in the southern city of Arequipa, rather than in the capital, Lima. The second limited the court's ability to examine the constitutionality of a law to a six-month window, beginning with the day the law was published in Peru's official legislative record (*Diario Oficial*). This amendment effectively prevented the court from examining all laws before January 1996. In other words, the court could not challenge the new constitution, the *auto-golpe*, Fujimori's past decree laws, or most of his controversial economic and human rights policies.

The Constitutional Court's most important decision involved Fujimori's right to a third election. Peru's 1993 constitution limited the president to a maximum of two consecutive terms. Yet the Fujimori-controlled Congress passed a law granting the president the right to run again in the 2000 election, and this law was challenged before the court. In a 5–2 ruling on January 17, 1997, the Constitutional Court declared the law unconstitutional; but because the ruling lacked a supermajority of justices, the law could not be struck from the books. However, three justices filed a separate opinion in which they held that Fujimori was constitutionally barred from seeking a third presidential term. These three justices, who had required a two-thirds congressional majority to be named, were then abruptly fired by a simple congressional majority in May.[36] In effect, after operating for less than a year, Peru's Constitutional Court was eliminated by Fujimori's administration when it proved to be an obstacle to the government's key interests.[37]

Fujimori's Meteoric Fall from Power and the Dismantling of Executive Dominance over Judicial Institutions

Peru's April 2000 national elections, criticized domestically and internationally for massive irregularities, resulted in a presidential runoff between Fujimori and the opposition candidate, Alejandro Toledo.[38] When the Peruvian government denied an Organization of American States (OAS) request to set up a monitoring system for the second round, Toledo opted to drop out of the race on May 18. Thus, running as the sole candidate, Fujimori was returned to the presidential palace for a third consecutive term on May 28, 2000. As Fujimori once again enjoyed a majority in the Peruvian Congress, he would continue to rule with few constraints.

In response to the events in Peru, and out of concern for the quality of democracy on the continent more generally, the Brazilian government hosted a reunion of South American presidents to discuss fortifying democratic rule in the region. "The Brasilia Agreement," the resulting document signed by Fujimori and eleven other presidents on September 1, 2000, included pledges to strengthen the independence of each country's judicial branch. As a show of good faith toward the Brasilia Accord, as well as a concession to U.S. pressure, the Peruvian government also agreed to engage in an OAS-sponsored national dialogue. Initiated on September 4, the dialogue was organized as a series of "Round Tables" (each composed of government, opposition, and civil society representatives) to discuss the reinvigoration of the country's democratic political institutions. The Round Table working group for the judiciary was to study judicial independence and the status of Peru's Constitutional Court.[39]

For most domestic observers, both the signing of the Brasilia Agreement and the OAS dialogue were viewed as superficial actions intended to placate Fujimori's internal and external critics. This sentiment was confirmed when Peru's Supreme Court chief justice announced—just three days after the formal inauguration of the September 4 OAS dialogue—that he was drafting a new law for the judiciary. Although he provided no details, as this chief justice was the very same individual who had previously relinquished judicial control to the executive branch, there was little expectation that executive control over the Peruvian judiciary was to be reversed. Instead, the forthcoming law was expected to renew the Executive Commission overseeing the judiciary (officially slated to expire in December 2000) and thereby extend Fujimori's dominance over the judiciary for the foreseeable future. However, following the president's abrupt loss of power one week later, any plans for this new judicial law were cut short.

On September 14, 2000, Lima's only remaining independent television station aired a video showing a Peruvian congressman accepting a bribe from Fujimori's chief adviser, Vladimir Montesinos.[40] (Montesinos fled the country shortly thereafter but was captured in Venezuela, and later tried in Peru and found guilty of corruption and human rights violations.) Fujimori, denying any knowledge of Montesinos's activities, announced two days later that he would be stepping down from office. In addition, Fujimori declared that a new presidential election, in which he would not be a candidate, would be held in 2001.[41] At the same time, however, Fujimori left the door open for his return to power in a subsequent presidential election in 2006. For example, when asked at a September 19, 2000, news conference about Peru's 2006 presidential election, Fujimori responded, "I've got a little surprise for you about what I'm going to do," clearly intimating his intent to return to the Peruvian presidential palace in the future (Rohter 2000, A14). Indeed, the day after Fujimori's news conference, *La Republica*'s headlines read I'M GOING, BUT I'M STAYING (Rohter 2000, A14).

Meanwhile, the OAS Round Table, as it was already coordinating talks between Fujimori's government and Peru's political opposition, began assisting Peru with its transition to a new government and return to democratic rule. However, while the Round Table could propose reforms, all suggested changes would still have to be passed by Peru's Congress—an institution still under Fujimori's control—and then signed into law by the president himself. Thus, Fujimori retained the final say over proposed changes.

With respect to the national judiciary, the Round Table proposed nullification of the law "equalizing" provisional magistrates on October 11, and this was passed by Congress two weeks later. On November 1, the Round Table proposed the deactivation of the judiciary's Executive Commission, and Congress approved this change two days later. It was immediately signed into law by Fujimori (Law 27367), thereby dismantling executive control of the judiciary.[42] The Round Table also proposed legislation to hold a special presidential election the following April and to prohibit immediate presidential re-election. Both of these were approved by the Fujimori-controlled Congress. Fujimori, having altered the constitution to allow his own re-election in 1995 and later assuming an illegal third term in 2000, now opted to revoke a president's right to a consecutive term.

While the transition negotiations were underway, a special ad hoc prosecutorial committee began investigating the revelations of corruption erupting against Fujimori's chief adviser. The Ad Hoc Committee discovered more than a thousand videos showing a large number of the country's most influential figures accepting bribes or otherwise engaging in compromising activities (Ugaz 2001). These scandals broadened to implicate Fujimori, and the president fled Peru on November 15. Four days later, Fujimori faxed his resignation from Tokyo and announced his intent to remain in Japan for the time being. The Peruvian Congress declared the vacancy of the presidency and chose Valentin Paniagua, then leader of the opposition in the legislature, as the country's interim president on November 21, 2000.

With Fujimori's flight, positive advancements rapidly occurred in the judicial branch. In late November, the National Magistrates Council and the Judicial Academy signed an agreement to terminate the high levels of provisional magistrates. The agreement stipulated that the academy would provide classes in December and the council would begin tenuring magistrates in January. Membership of a new temporary council for the judiciary was reached on December 4, and the nominees were esteemed members of the judicial branch. A new Supreme Court chief justice was selected on December 7. The following week the president of the Constitutional Court announced plans to reduce the number of votes required to declare a law unconstitutional to a simple majority from six out of seven. Congress also dismantled the "temporary courts," such as the anti-drug and penal courts, which the government had used to protect its allies and harass its opponents. In February 2001, due to the allegations of murder, embezzlement, and dereliction of duty against Fujimori, Congress banned the former president from holding public office for ten years, or until 2011. Although Fujimori had already stated that he would not be a candidate in the 2001 election, this law would bar him from running for the presidency in 2006.

The April 8, 2001, special presidential election resulted in a runoff in June, with the second round won by Alejandro Toledo, who pledged to rebuild Peru's democratic institutions. Following the election, the names of many of the country's most respected legal figures were circulated as potential candidates to fill key judicial positions, such as the attorney general and the minister of justice (Ugaz 2001). While in power, the Toledo administration continued to press for Fujimori's extradition to Peru to stand charges on corruption and human rights violations. The Japanese government, however, awarded Fujimori "honorary citizenship" and refused to comply.

Fujimori, from his website in Japan and weekly radio program broadcast in Peru, claimed to be innocent of all twenty-two charges against him and repeatedly declared his intent to return to Peru in 2006 as that country's elected president.[43] At a press conference in Tokyo on October 6, 2005, Fujimori officially announced he would run for the Peruvian presidency the following April. That same day Fujimori's defense lawyers stated that they were confident that Peru's courts would drop the arrest orders against him and thereby allow Fujimori to return to Peru to inaugurate his candidacy (Hayes 2005). His lawyers also stated that they were preparing a challenge to the congressional ban that barred Fujimori from holding public office. One month later, in early November, Fujimori unexpectedly showed up in Chile and was arrested at his hotel by Chilean authorities.[44] Losing his bid to be set free, Fujimori remained under arrest while Peru formally prepared its extradition request. On January 6, 2006, Fujimori's daughter registered his candidacy with Peru's National Electoral Board, the institution that has final authority over candidates, in Lima. The board rejected his candidacy, and Fujimori was unable to participate in Peru's April 2006 presidential election. As of June 2007, Fujimori remained detained in Santiago, awaiting the decision of a Chilean Supreme Court judge on whether he will be extradited to Peru.

Explaining Peru's Pattern of Judicial Reform: Initiation Versus Implementation

In 1990, when Fujimori assumed office, he was constitutionally barred from seeking a consecutive presidential term. Only by amending Peru's constitution, a process that was set in motion with the 1992 *golpe* and the constitutional convention that followed, could he obtain the right to a second presidential bid. Fujimori's original constitutional proposals—which included allowing executive intervention in the naming of all magistrates and the elimination of Peru's Constitutional Court—sought to weaken the judiciary. However, as the constitution had to be approved in a national referendum, and the general public appeared unwilling to support it without institutional protections to strengthen the judiciary, Fujimori was compelled to cede judicial advances to ensure the constitution's ratification. In effect, in exchange for agreeing to judicial empowerment, the president received the right to re-election, a specific and immediate benefit.

In addition, the initiation of judicial reform provided Fujimori with another significant benefit: it pleased the international community. Both multilateral organizations and foreign governments had called for the increased independence of the Peruvian judicial branch. While international development organizations emphasized the relationship among judicial independence, investor confidence, and economic performance, foreign governments expressed concern for democratization and human rights. Thus, the Peruvian government's constitutional pledges to strengthen the country's judicial institutions were favorably received by actors in the international community.

While the initiation of judicial reform had direct benefits for Fujimori, it also entailed potential costs. Specifically, if Fujimori were forced to implement judicial reform so as to empower the courts, the resulting judiciary could check his authority. However, since implementation would remain at the president's discretion, Fujimori could control the laws that would flesh out the restructured judiciary. Because the implementation of agreed-upon changes remained under Fujimori's control, the implied costs of initiating judicial reform were greatly discounted by the president. Realizing that it could later boycott these institutions, the government readily agreed to increases in judicial autonomy and to the re-establishment of the Constitutional Court at the constitutional convention (Borea Odria 1996, 11). Thus, in the eyes of Fujimori at the first stage of reform, the immediate benefits of judicial reform easily outweighed the potential costs, and initiation was successfully achieved.

However, once Fujimori obtained the right to re-election, his perspective on judicial reform underwent a dramatic transformation. Instead of implementing the judicial advancements promised in his new constitution, Fujimori oversaw legislation to erase all judicial autonomy. Beginning with his control over the temporary Congress, Fujimori undermined the National Magistrates Council, the Judicial Academy, and the Constitutional Court. After Fujimori's 1995 re-election, the president's attacks on the judicial apparatus became more aggressive (Cubas 1997b). The judiciary's Executive Commission, controlled by Fujimori, usurped the powers of both the National Magistrates Council and the Judicial Academy. The government also dismembered the Constitutional Court, firing three justices just six months after its inception, leaving the court without the necessary quorum to bring down laws.

With his return to the presidential palace in 1995 for another five-year term, Fujimori had no incentive to follow through with meaningful judicial reform. Implementing such reform in the spirit of the 1993 constitution would have meant accepting judicial limits on Fujimori's power. Thus, the cost of following through with initiated reforms was high. At the same time, the president had nothing more to gain from continuing on with judicial reform: granting the courts real independence would not provide additional benefits. By agreeing to constitutionally empower the judiciary, Fujimori had received the right to re-election. That benefit was now exhausted. As Fujimori was already enjoying his second term, he could not obtain additional benefits from upholding his half of the constitutional bargain.

Not only could Fujimori see no additional benefit from proceeding with judicial reform, but the punishment for nonimplementation was negligible: failure to comply with his earlier constitutional pledges did not result in the imposition of penalties. While domestic sources vociferously criticized the government's manipulation of judicial institutions, this criticism had little impact on the president's political power. Likewise, the international community was equally ineffective at forcing the government to make progress on its promised judicial advancements. For example, while the United States criticized the Fujimori administration for establishing the Executive Commission and for firing the Constitutional Court justices, this did not affect U.S. economic assistance to Peru.

As for the IFIs, they continued to supply funds to Peru for judicial reform, even after it became blatantly obvious that the Peruvian government had no interest in respecting judicial autonomy. Both the Inter-American Development Bank and the World Bank signed judicial reform loan agreements with the Peruvian government in late 1997 (for US$20 million and US$22.5 million, respectively).[45] These loans were granted even though the Executive Commission had controlled the judicial branch since 1995 and the Constitutional Court justices had been fired in January 1997. Although the World Bank's loan was terminated in 1998 due to political intervention in the judiciary, no other World Bank funding was affected (Montoya Anguerry 1998). From the president's point of view, failing to implement promised judicial reform had few negative consequences: Fujimori only forfeited loans for the specific purpose of judicial empowerment, a purpose that he had no interest in seeing realized.

With his 2000 second re-election, Fujimori was set to renew the Executive Commission and retain his control over the judicial branch. As he returned to power for another five years, his priority was to maintain a subordinate judiciary. However, once Fujimori announced that he was giving up the presidency following the September 2000 corruption scandal, his judicial strategy changed dramatically. In the period immediately following Fujimori's resignation, Congress enacted legislation to rescind executive dominance over the judicial branch. At that time, Fujimori still controlled the Peruvian Congress; *he could have prevented the passage of legislation to reinstate judicial independence.* Yet he chose not to do so. Instead, in the days preceding his flight to Japan, Fujimori oversaw a rapid reversal of his earlier judicial legislation. The president himself, who had spent the last ten years destroying judicial autonomy, now signed into law the very changes that would undo executive control over the judicial branch.

When it was clear that he would not be remaining in power, the president suddenly found it in his interest to remove the judiciary from executive control. Fujimori's judicial tactics make sense considering that the president was stepping down from power with an eye toward returning to office in the future. While Fujimori would not be a candidate in the immediate special election, he left no doubt about his intent to campaign for the presidency in 2006. From Fujimori's perspective, the establishment of an independent judiciary would both protect the policies he had put in place and establish checks on Peru's incoming president. Independent courts could also prevent his successor from attempting to bar Fujimori from returning to the presidential palace at a later date. Thus, after having eviscerated Peru's judicial autonomy during the course of his presidential tenure, Fujimori—upon leaving office—returned to the judicial branch the independence originally granted to it in the 1993 constitution.

The Peruvian case fits a pattern that was also followed by Argentina in the 1990s. In both cases, presidents traded judicial empowerment for the right to re-election. Upon re-election, each president subsequently lost interest in completing promised judicial advances. In consequence, initiated reforms faltered at implementation, and the judicial branch was effectively prevented from challenging presidential power. In both countries the emergence of the necessary political will to strengthen the judiciary coincided with the reversal of the president's political fortunes. Only once Fujimori and Menem perceived their probability of retaining power to be disappearing did they seek to rescind executive domination over the judiciary. In both Peru and Argentina the presidents still controlled Congress and could have prevented such changes but did not. Instead, they oversaw the passage of legislation to strengthen judicial independence. Thus, while Menem and Fujimori refused to accept judicial limitations on their own authority, their decision to release the judiciary from executive control makes sense given their loss of political power.

Chapter Four

Judicial Reform in Mexico in the 1990s

Immediately on taking office in December 1994, President Ernesto Zedillo delivered to the Mexican Congress a comprehensive judicial reform
package of dramatic constitutional changes affecting the independence
and authority of the judicial branch. The Supreme Court was granted the
power of judicial review in specifically defined circumstances and was
also empowered to settle political controversies between and among the
branches of government at federal, state, and local levels. As a result of
the reforms, the Mexican judiciary, subordinate to the Mexican president
and his Institutional Revolutionary Party (PRI) for the past sixty-seven
years, apparently was now being positioned as an effective counterweight
capable of checking the power of the ruling party. Just five months later
the PRI-controlled Congress fully implemented these institutional reforms as envisioned by the December constitutional changes. In 1998, less
than four years after the reforms took effect, Mexico's restructured Supreme Court ruled against the PRI on a key political issue, clearly demonstrating that the reforms had fundamentally altered the traditional
balance of power between Mexico's executive and judicial branches.

Why would the Mexican president seek to create a Supreme Court
capable of declaring the laws enacted under his administration unconstitutional? Furthermore, why would the president seek to create a court capable of resolving disputes over the rightful boundaries of political power
between government offices held by opposition parties and those held by
the ruling party? I argue that while Mexico's 1994 judicial reform appears
puzzling on the surface, it makes sense when understood as a political

"insurance policy" designed to protect a weakening ruling party that found itself unable to control political outcomes as it had in the past. Operating in an increasingly insecure political arena, the ruling party had the incentive not only to initiate judicial reform, but to implement it as well. Thus, unlike its counterparts in Argentina and in Peru, the ruling party followed through with judicial empowerment.

The first section in this chapter describes the long-standing institutional weakness of the Mexican judiciary under the PRI. The second section details the constitutional changes initiated under Zedillo's judicial reform package. The next section summarizes Mexico's straightforward process of implementation. It then documents postreform Supreme Court rulings, thereby demonstrating the newly acquired power of Mexico's restructured judicial branch. Finally, the last section analyzes the reform and argues that the PRI, facing a decreasing likelihood of retaining control over political offices, opted to allow the reforms to be meaningfully implemented.

The Mexican Judiciary Under PRI Hegemony

Although the last two decades of the twentieth century marked a period of democratic transition in Mexico, culminating in the election of the opposition candidate Vicente Fox in the 2000 presidential election, Mexico at the time of the 1994 judicial reform was perhaps best described as a "semiauthoritarian democracy."[1] The Mexican Constitution of 1917, from which the past and current federal government derives its authority, formally establishes a democratic government based on the separation of powers. For most of the last century, however, Mexican politics was characterized by *presidencialismo* and a hegemonic party system (Camp 1993). The Mexican president, both head of government and head of the PRI, effectively monopolized political power, tightly controlled access to office and policy decisions, and dominated the existing institutional checks (Weldon 1997).[2]

The judiciary in particular was traditionally a subordinate institution. The weakness of Mexico's judiciary reflected three features of the Mexican political system, including repeated executive intervention, presidential control over selection and careers, and the court's formal lack of judicial review powers. First, the federal judicial branch was subjected to a multiplicity of constitutional revisions. These reforms, introduced by successive presidents, marked the branch with institutional instability and eviscerated the promises of judicial independence enshrined in the 1917 constitution.[3] In 1928, President Calles fired and renamed the entire Supreme Court. Amending the constitution, he granted presidents the right to nominate justices while simultaneously reducing ratification requirements to a simple Senate majority. The following president once again replaced all members of the court, fixed the terms of justices to coincide with the presidential *sexenio,* and abolished life tenure. In addition, these early presidents also incrementally augmented the size of the bench from eleven to twenty-six justices. Life tenure was restored in 1944, but by that time "the tone of executive-judicial relations had been set . . . a compliant court had been consolidated" (Domingo 2000, 713).

Second, both the judicial selection process and political career structure left justices beholden to the president and ruling party in a one-party-dominant political system (Domingo 2000). From 1934 to 1994, since the president's hand-picked candidate was readily confirmed by the PRI-controlled Senate, each Mexican president was able to shape the composition of his court (Magaloni and Sánchez 2001, 3). As the selection and career advancement of lower-level judges was in the hands of the Supreme Court, judicial dependence replicated down the judicial ladder (Cossío-Díaz 1998a).[4] Furthermore, justices frequently saw the court as a stepping-stone to a better political post, not as an end in itself, and therefore had reasons to toe the party line. For example, for retired justices on whom there is data available, nearly one quarter of them were immediately placed in upper-echelon political posts (Magaloni and Sánchez 2001, 6).[5] Before the 1994 reform, justices remained on the court about ten years on average, with justices chosen from outside the judicial branch particularly likely to abandon the court for more attractive political positions (Cossío-Díaz 1998a). Thus, the incentive system encouraged rulings favorable to the president and ruling party, and it is no surprise that justices assiduously avoided politically sensitive issues (Fix-Fierro 1998; Domingo 2000; Magaloni and Sánchez 2001).[6]

Finally, the Supreme Court's formal lack of judicial review undermined the possibility of judicial constraints on the unconstitutional use of political authority in Mexico. Prior to the 1994 reform, the Mexican legal system recognized *amparo* (protection of individual guarantees) as the sole mechanism available to challenge the constitutionality of a law. Under *amparo,* a court's ruling has effect only for the individual bringing the case, not for the entire population. Thus, even if a judge finds a law to be unconstitutional in an *amparo* suit, the judge's decision does not abrogate the law because judicial rulings are denied general effects. According to former chief justice Juventino Castro y Castro, "There is no such thing as *amparo* against unconstitutional laws; there is only *amparo* against the application of such laws to a specific case which has been raised by an individual who has been diligent enough to request it from the Federal Judiciary" (quoted in Estrada Samano 1995, 44). Furthermore, *amparo* was additionally weakened because Mexican presidents restricted the issues that could be brought under such suits and because the Supreme Court avoided using the *amparo* to challenge presidents on critical political or financial matters (Domingo 2000; Fix-Fierro 1998).[7]

An explicitly clear assessment of the traditional relationship between the executive and judiciary in Mexico was revealed by President Zedillo when he declared in his 1995 State of the Union Address, "I reiterate that the times of political naming of the Court and presidential influence over the Supreme Court have ended" (Zedillo 1995). Throughout the nearly three-quarters of a century of PRI rule, judges were unable and unwilling to serve as effective restraints on either the executive branch or the ruling party. In 1994, after numerous prior constitutional changes and Supreme Court packings, the judicial branch was once again renamed and restructured by executive intervention.

The 1994 Mexican Judicial Reform Bill

On December 5, 1994, President Zedillo introduced in Congress a comprehensive package of constitutional reforms that altered the Supreme Court, created a federal judicial council (CFJ), and granted the high court judicial review powers. Like all constitutional revisions in Mexico, these changes needed to be approved by a majority of state legislatures as well as by two-thirds of both the Senate and the Chamber of Deputies. While the president was easily able to command approval by state legislatures and the Senate (where his party held more than two-thirds of the seats), the PRI possessed just a simple majority in the lower house. Needing additional votes in order to pass his constitutional proposals in the Chamber of Deputies, Zedillo sought the support of the PAN (National Action Party). Thus, the initiation of Mexico's 1994 judicial reform was achieved by a PRI-PAN coalition. The final version of these constitutional changes was published in Mexico's *Diario Oficial* on December 31 and subsequently took effect on January 1, 2005.

The Supreme Court

With regard to the high court, the constitutional revisions altered the composition of the Supreme Court and the selection of its justices. The total number of seats on the bench was reduced from twenty-six to eleven, thereby returning the court to the number of members originally established by the 1917 constitution, and the sitting justices were immediately retired. As for choosing justices, the Senate now selects one candidate from a list of three names sent by the president and the confirmation of this nominee requires the approval of two-thirds of the Senate (rather than a simple majority as before). Although the PRI still enjoyed a two-thirds grip on the Senate in 1994, it was unlikely that any one party would be able to do so for much longer. Hence, the change promotes the appointment of nonpartisan justices as no one party would be able to single-handedly name its own candidate in the future. Furthermore, the prerequisites for nominating justices were made more rigorous and candidates must now possess more extensive professional experience. Prospective justices must also face Senate interviews before confirmation and cannot have held a major political post in the year preceding their nomination. Both more demanding credentials required of nominees and public scrutiny of their qualifications during Senate hearings favor candidates with greater expertise. On the negative side, however, the reform replaced the life tenure of justices with fifteen-year, staggered terms. The decrease in security of office undermines a key safeguard of justices' impartiality, especially as younger justices will be compelled to retire from the court at an age when they may still be in the job market and seeking career advancement.

In addition to these formal institutional changes, two nonstructural variables have significant implications for the independence of Mexico's twenty-first-century Supreme Court. The first is the country's changing domestic political environment in which the demise of one-party politics has altered the incentive structure for Supreme Court justices (Domingo 2000). A justice can no longer be certain that a future president, at a time when the justice might seek another political office, will belong to a particular party. Because of this contingency, the best course of action for a justice may no longer be to issue legal rulings in the hope of currying favor with the government. The second important nonstructural change is the selection of justices who are dedicated to a career in the judiciary. The naming of justices who view a seat on the Supreme Court as the pinnacle of their career, rather than as a strategic move to a more coveted political office, provides justices with the incentive to foster the prestige of the Mexican Supreme Court.

The Federal Judicial Council

Both lower-level judicial selection and judicial administration had previously been the Supreme Court's responsibility, but the 1994 reform transferred these responsibilities to the newly created Federal Judicial Council (CFJ). Mexico's CFJ is a seven-member body composed of the country's chief justice, three lower-level judges, two members chosen by the Senate, and one member appointed by the president. The members serve four-year, nonrenewable terms. Zedillo's original proposal had called for two representatives appointed by the president (and just two instead of three lower-level judges), but the final draft approved by Congress reduced the president's selection to one member (Fix-Zamudio and Cossío-Díaz 1996, 549). Although the designation process for judicial appointments was left vague in 1994 (Aranda 1999), as a result of constitutional reforms pushed by the Supreme Court in 1999, it is now the court that is responsible for selecting the CFJ's three lower-level judicial representatives. The council's mixed membership, a majority of which is chosen from the judicial branch, makes it difficult for any external influence to manipulate the council's decisions for political gain.

In order to promote judicial independence, the CFJ is vested with key responsibilities over judicial careers, including the appointment, promotion, and discipline of all judges below the Supreme Court level. Rather than have lower-level judges appointed by the Supreme Court, as was the case prior to the reform, now a nonpartisan council determines the selection and promotion of these judges. Furthermore, the council is charged with the professionalization of the national judiciary and the establishment of prerequisites for judicial careers (university curriculum and standards for advancement based on experience and merit evaluations). The CFJ's use of established merit evaluations to determine career advancement means that a judge's prospects will depend on a demonstrated competency rather than on connections or political ties. The council's responsibility for the discipline and life tenure ratification of lower-level judges also provides for improved judicial insulation, thereby allowing judges to decide cases contrary to the wishes of those with political power or social influence without fear of retribution.[8] Furthermore, increasing regard for professionalization, greater experience requirements for advancement, and establishment of a specialized curriculum should lead to a more qualified cadre of judges.

The creation of a special council to oversee the judiciary's broad range of administrative functions is also a positive step in the development of judicial autonomy. The CFJ, because it establishes territorial divisions and the number of circuits, enjoys the ability to determine the total number of judges. Responsibility for preparing the judicial branch's budget, which was also transferred from the Supreme Court to the council, enables the CFJ to oversee the setting of priorities and allocation of resources within the judicial branch.[9] The CFJ submits its budget to the president who then refers it to Congress as part of the national budget proposal.[10] While the Supreme Court does retain some administrative functions, the CFJ is now the main body charged with judicial administration, and the high court is primarily responsible for issuing rulings to resolve disputes and to determine the constitutionality of laws.[11]

Judicial Review Powers

The most significant changes brought about by Mexico's 1994 judicial reform bill involve the political understanding surrounding the Supreme Court's role as a check in the separation of powers. This change is embodied in the court's right to resolve "constitutional controversies" and to determine the "unconstitutionality of laws."[12] Supreme Court decisions in these two areas have the potential to have "general effects"; in other words, they may declare government acts (in the first instance) or laws (in the second) as null and void. Thus, by establishing the general effects of Supreme Court decisions in cases involving "constitutional controversies" or "unconstitutionality of laws," Mexico's 1994 judicial reform granted the Supreme Court the right to act as a constitutional court capable of controlling the constitutionality of government actions and laws.

The term *constitutional controversies* refers to the Supreme Court's right to resolve conflicts between public entities in which one entity alleges the other's infringement on a mutual jurisdiction. These conflicts include disputes between the president and Congress, between the federal government and states or cities, between two states, between political organs within states, and between states and cities. Any of these entities may petition the court to hear its case. Although the Supreme Court did previously enjoy the ability to decide such controversies, its decisions did not have any effect beyond the immediate parties involved. Now, the Supreme Court may void an act or law if it is found to violate the jurisdiction of another official public entity.

The explicit inclusion of cities on the list of entities with legal standing to request review is another innovation. In the past, the status of cities under this clause was ambiguous, and varied depending on the prevailing political winds. With formal inclusion in the constitutional controversies clause, cities now possess a clearly defined right to seek legal recourse against presumed unconstitutional acts contrary to their interests.

The 1994 reform also granted the Mexican Supreme Court a second, entirely new function as a constitutional court via the unconstitutionality of laws clause. Mexico's Supreme Court may now invalidate laws passed by Congress, state legislatures, and Mexico City's legislative assembly. The court may examine the constitutional validity of a law if one-third of the members of the legislature that passed the law petition the court to do so. While Zedillo's initial constitutional proposal stipulated a minimum support level of 45 percent of the members of a legislature to challenge a law, Congress reduced this requirement to just 33 percent (Fix-Zamudio and Cossío-Díaz 1996, 549). In addition to legislative petitions, under this clause the Senate may request the court to review the constitutionality of treaties, and the attorney general may request Supreme Court examination of any law passed by national, state, or local legislatures.[13]

Both the constitutional controversies and the unconstitutionality of laws clauses enable the Supreme Court to limit governmental authority and define political boundaries, thereby increasing the importance of the judiciary as a mechanism for constitutional control. However, the court's new power to check unconstitutional government action is severely limited in several ways. First, the agreement of a supermajority of justices (eight out of eleven, or 72 percent) is required to invalidate an unconstitutional act or law under either of the two constitutional control clauses.[14] Zedillo's initiative would have required a supermajority of nine justices, but this was decreased to eight by Congress. Furthermore, with respect to constitutional controversies, the court's ruling will have general effects only when a higher body challenges a lower-level one; for example, when a federal body challenges a state or municipal one. Should a lower body challenge a higher body and win with the approval of at least eight justices, the court ruling will apply only to the lower body involved in that particular case, as was the norm before the reforms. Likewise, the supermajority stipulation applies to unconstitutional laws; the Supreme Court can declare a law null and void only when eight out of eleven justices agree on the unconstitutionality of the law in question. Thus, even if a majority of justices (six or seven) on the court were to declare a law in violation of an individual's constitutional rights, the law would continue in effect.

The 1994 reform placed two additional restrictions on the court's power to invalidate laws via the unconstitutional laws clause. First, members of any legislature who desire to question the constitutionality of a law passed by their assembly have only thirty days from the publication of the law to file a petition with the court. Second, the court was explicitly prohibited from using the unconstitutionality of laws clause to determine the constitutionality of laws with respect to "electoral matters." The new 1994 judicial reform specifically states that the court cannot decide whether electoral laws are constitutional. The opposition therefore would be unable to challenge electoral rules constructed to provide advantages to the PRI. (For example, such rules allocated 74 percent of the seats in the Senate to the PRI even though it had received only 48 percent of the vote.)[15] Mexico's 1996 electoral reform, passed two years after Mexico's judicial reform was promulgated, partly removed this limitation by allowing for electoral cases to be taken under the unconstitutional laws clause.[16] The court, however, may only examine the validity of the parts of the electoral law challenged and may not extend its ruling to cover constitutional issues that are not formally brought by the petitioners.[17]

The Mexican Supreme Court's explicit empowerment to act as a constitutional court is a fundamental change in Mexico's separation of powers (Melgar Adalid 1998). Via the constitutional controversies and unconstitutional laws clauses, the Supreme Court has the potential to define political boundaries and declare unconstitutional laws null and void. Nevertheless, the requirement of a supermajority to achieve a ruling with general effects means that the court's ability to overturn government acts and laws is still discouraged rather than encouraged. If an act or law continues to have legal authority even though seven Supreme Court justices find that it violates constitutional principles, this outcome may undermine respect for judicial authority. The thirty-day limit for members of the legislature to petition the Supreme Court to examine the constitutionality of a law is a very short time, both to prepare a legal challenge and simply to discover the law's effects. This time constraint makes it impossible to challenge laws that result in unfair consequences over time. More important, this time limit effectively favors the PRI, because all laws passed during the period of PRI dominance before the 1994 judicial reform were excluded from challenges of unconstitutionality because they were, by definition, outside the thirty-day time period.[18]

Implementation and Postreform Supreme Court Rulings: Evidence of an Empowered Judiciary

The constitutional reforms initiated in Mexico in December 1994 were followed soon thereafter with the full implementation of these judicial advancements. Implementation was completed via the passage of two pieces of congressional legislation, the Ley Reglamentaria and the Ley Orgánica del Poder Judicial de la Federación. These laws, published in the *Diario Oficial* on May 11, 1995, and May 26, 1995, respectively (Fix-

Zamudio and Cossío-Díaz 1996, 558 and 566), filled in specific details of the restructured judicial branch (for example, the term of the Mexican Supreme Court chief justice).[19] Most important, they upheld the changes to judicial independence and Supreme Court power established at initiation. As this legislation required only the approval of a simple majority in each house, a level of support possessed by the PRI, implementation remained at the discretion of the ruling party. In this case, the ruling party chose to implement judicial reform, shortly after initiation and in a straightforward manner, in the spirit of the constitutional revisions.

At the time of the reform, some critics claimed that this judicial reform was purely cosmetic and would not alter the historic impotence of the judicial branch. Thus, the question arises, were these latest changes truly substantive, as is claimed here? An examination of post-1994 decisions provides concrete evidence that Mexico's new Supreme Court is both willing and able to rule against the president and ruling party.

The first exercise of the court's new judicial review powers against the PRI occurred in 1998, only four years after Mexico's judicial reform, when the Supreme Court declared unconstitutional an electoral law intended to maintain PRI dominance in the state of Quintana Roo.[20] PRI legislators, realizing that they would lose control over the Quintana Roo state legislature in the next election, enacted a new state electoral law, known as the "governability clause," which would have awarded a majority of legislative seats to the plurality vote winner. Because the PRI expected to garner the largest share of the vote but still under 40 percent, the clause would have guaranteed the PRI's continued unilateral control over the Quintana Roo legislature even though it polled less than a majority of the vote. In response to the passage of the governability clause, legislators from the opposition Party of the Democratic Revolution (PRD) filed an unconstitutional laws petition with the Supreme Court in August 1998 to challenge the legality of the state's new electoral code. In a unanimous ruling, all eleven justices declared the clause to be unconstitutional. As a result, the law was struck from the state's electoral code, and the PRI's monopoly over political power in Quintana Roo was broken.[21]

Not only has the court been willing to challenge the PRI at the state level, but the justices have also used their newly acquired judicial review powers to rule against the political elite at the federal level, including the previously sacrosanct presidency. The first challenge to be filed against a Mexican president under the judiciary's new constitutional control powers was brought by the federal Congress against Zedillo under constitutional controversies in 1999. At that time, members of Congress from the National Action Party (PAN) and the PRD were attempting to conduct an investigation of alleged illicit bank financing of PRI candidates during the 1994 election, including the funding of Zedillo's presidential campaign. They were stymied by a recalcitrant executive branch.[22] PAN and PRD legislators petitioned the court to determine whether the president was obligated to deliver the requested secret banking data to Congress. On August 25, 2000, in another unanimous decision, the justices ordered Zedillo to remand the relevant documents to Congress within thirty days. Zedillo, now at the end of his *sexenio*, complied with the ruling; the secretary of the treasury and the head of the National Banking Commission delivered the requested files on time. In this case it may be argued that a lame duck president was too weak to ward off judicial encroachment. But the Supreme Court has been just as able to counter the interests of Vicente Fox, even at the beginning of his presidential term.

The first major judicial challenge faced by Fox began with a dispute between the PAN president and the PRD mayor of Mexico City, Andrés Manuel López Obrador, over the implementation of daylight saving time. Annual presidential decrees had established daylight saving time in Mexico since 1996. The executive branch justified the time change by arguing that the additional hour of daylight saved hundreds of millions of pesos in energy costs and also brought Mexico in line with the United States, the country's most important economic partner. López Obrador, stating that daylight saving disrupted people's biological clocks, announced in March 2001 that Mexico City would not implement the time change and used constitutional controversies to challenge the president's right to do so. In an eight-to-two decision (only ten of the eleven justices voted in this ruling) on April 6, the justices ruled against the mayor, claiming that the setting of time was a federal prerogative. However, the decision left unresolved the question of which federal branch was legally empowered to determine the Mexican time. In a second ruling on this issue, on September 4, 2001, the court unanimously decided against the Mexican president, with all eleven justices agreeing that the setting of the clocks was a congressional responsibility. Congress did pass daylight saving legislation the following February, although its version of the law implemented the time change for seven months rather than the six months originally established by presidential decree.

Yet another Supreme Court ruling worth examining declared unconstitutional a presidential decree allowing for private participation in the provision of electrical energy for public use. President Fox had made reforming Mexico's energy sector a key priority of his administration. His Public Service Electric Energy Law, decreed on May 22, 2001, would have allowed large corporations producing electricity for their own use to sell any surplus they generated to the state for redistribution to the general public. However, Article 28 of the Mexican constitution reserves energy as a state monopoly, with the state solely responsible for the generation, transmission, and distribution of electricity. In addition, energy privatization is strongly opposed by both the PRD and elements of the PRI, and it was congressional members of these two parties who filed a constitutional controversies petition challenging the legality of the decree law. In an eight-to-three ruling on April 25, 2002, the Supreme Court held that the presidential decree was unconstitutional, thereby ruling out the possibility that the Federal Electricity Commission could purchase surplus electricity from private providers and dealing a blow to one of the centerpieces of Fox's agenda.

Finally, the Supreme Court's power also depends on its willingness to rule on issues it may have avoided addressing in the past. In this regard, the reformed court has greatly expanded the range of its jurisdictional powers. The court has been ruling on issues that are hotly contested and highly controversial—issues that previously would have been decided behind closed doors by the ruling party elite. Besides the political matters mentioned above, the high court has also ruled on an array of economic and social issues, including allowing the capitalization of interest on bank debt; the unconstitutionality of the luxury tax; the right of entrepreneurs to refuse membership in government-sponsored chambers of commerce; the federal government's right to audit the national university; the fining of the state-owned oil company, PEMEX, for a spill on the Gulf coast; the denial of extradition to the United States of alleged criminals who could face the death penalty (capital punishment is illegal in Mexico); the right of living individuals to sell their organs for transplants; and the decriminalization of abortion in cases of rape or severe fetal deformity.

The court's decisions, as well as the broad range of issues on which it has ruled, provide evidence of a fundamentally restructured relationship between Mexico's traditional wielders of political power and its judicial branch. With rulings against the PRI, as well as against both PRI and PAN presidents, Mexico's postreform Supreme Court has clearly demonstrated both an ability and a willingness to enter the political fray.

Initiation Followed by Meaningful Implementation: Explaining Mexico's 1994 Judicial Reform

The Mexican experience with implementation contrasts sharply with the implementation experiences of Argentina and Peru in the 1990s. Unlike Argentina and Peru, where ruling parties used implementation to undermine judicial empowerment, Mexico saw implementation that affirmed the positive judicial changes established under the new constitution. Why was Zedillo willing to enact reforms that Menem and Fujimori actively sought to block?

By the early 1990s, Mexico's president and ruling party had an interest in creating institutional mechanisms to protect themselves, given the likelihood that PRI power would continue to diminish. Zedillo initiated the reform process, defined the parameters of the debate, and specifically tailored the Supreme Court's two new powers of judicial review to protect the ruling party where it perceived itself to be the most vulnerable. In the Mexican case, the PRI had the incentive to follow through with the implementation of judicial advances proclaimed in the revised constitution. However, the PRI did not have the congressional votes necessary to alter the country's constitution unilaterally and therefore was forced to seek the support of the PAN. In exchange for its support, the PAN demanded the establishment of a judiciary stronger than that which Zedillo had originally proposed. The combination of an insecure ruling party seeking insurance and an opposition party pushing for greater judicial empowerment determined the final judicial reform package.

The PRI and Domestic Political Uncertainty

The PRI had dominated Mexican politics since 1929, making it one of the longest-ruling single-party governments in the world. Traditionally the PRI had used economic growth to legitimate its rule and to obtain votes. Where the PRI could not achieve victory by legitimate means, it resorted to electoral manipulation. By the mid-1990s, both of these strategies were under fire. A debt crisis was undermining PRI hegemony and fundamentally altering Mexico's domestic political arena. Economic stagnation was further weakening the PRI's hold on power, and the presence of international observers to monitor elections reduced the party's ability to retain power through electoral fraud. The opposition, meanwhile, made headway in opening up the country's political playing field. The two most important opposition parties by the mid-1990s were the PAN on the right of the political spectrum and the left-leaning PRD, which began as a coalition of minor parties in the 1988 presidential election.

Table 1.
Mexican Presidential Election Results by Candidate, 1970–1994

Year	PRI	PAN	PRD/FDN*
1970	83.3	13.9	—
1976	100.0	—	—
1982	71.0	15.7	—
1988	50.3	17.0	31.1
1994	48.7	25.9	16.6

* The National Democratic Front (FDN) was an electoral coalition uniting small parties on the left behind the PRD's candidate in 1988 and 1994.
Source: *Statistical Abstract of Latin America* 2002.

Mexican electoral trends from 1970 to 1994 are demonstrated in table 1, which shows the decrease in the (official) vote received by the PRI presidential candidate over the twenty-five years, from 93.6 percent in 1976 to 48.7 percent in 1994. In the June 1994 presidential election, opposition parties garnered more than 50 percent of the electorate's votes. The PAN chairman, following the party's strong showing, stated that the PAN was establishing as its goals "a majority in Congress in the 1997 elections and then the presidency in the year 2000" (Romero 1995, 12). After the 1994 results, the PRI had to take such election bravado seriously.

With respect to congressional representation, the opposition made only token advances in membership until 1994. As the PRI had always maintained two-thirds of both houses in Congress, it had long been able to legislate unilaterally and to engage in constitutional revisions at will. In the 1994 congressional election, the PRI received a two-thirds majority in the Senate but retained only a simple majority in the Chamber of Deputies. In consequence, the PRI no longer possessed the necessary two-thirds majority in the lower house required to approve changes to Mexico's constitution. Thus, for the first time, the proportion of seats held by opposition parties in Congress began to have important consequences.

Paralleling changes at the federal level, political power at state and local levels in Mexico had also become increasingly diversified by 1994. The PRI was contending with opposition strongholds in the north (the PAN) and in the south (the PRD) and with weak electoral support in Mexico City. Members of the opposition had successfully competed against the PRI for governorships and seats in state legislatures, for political offices in the capital city, and for positions at the local level. The first non-PRI governor, a member of the PAN, came to power in Baja California in 1988, and two more PAN governors were elected in 1994.

This trend of increasing opposition control of political office and concomitant loss of the PRI's control over those offices continued with the elections of 1997 and 2000. In the July 1997 congressional election, the ruling party lost its majority in the Chamber of Deputies. Hence, the PRI would now be unable to pass legislation without first building a coalition with another party in the lower house. The mayoralty of Mexico City, decided by popular election rather than appointment for the first time in 1997, was won by the PRD's candidate, Cuauhtémoc Cárdenas. In addition, eight governorships were held by opposition parties, including seven by the PAN and one by the PRD, and the opposition also controlled several state legislatures (see Instituto Nacional de Geografía e Informática 1999, 623). Opposition parties also came to control one-third of all municipalities (Blum 1997, 28–42). In 2000 the PRI lost the presidency to the PAN candidate, Vicente Fox, heralding a fundamental change in the Mexican political system.

Thus, while as late as the end of Miguel de la Madrid's presidency (1982), guests at a PRI dinner party were discussing their political plans for the PRI's next four *sexenios* in power (Solis 1994, A1), by 1994 that situation had clearly changed. In the elections of 1994, "the PRI was seen for the first time as vulnerable to growing voter discontent and a new element, uncertainty, entered the electoral scene" (Serrano 1994, 12). In the week following the election that brought President Zedillo to power, the *Wall Street Journal's* correspondent in Mexico was writing, "In the new disorder of Mexican politics, the nation's ruling party is no longer the reassuring but undemocratic absolute" (Solis 1994, A1). After nearly seven decades in power, the ruling party had lost its unilateral control over decision making. Furthermore, the PRI could now no longer unequivocally predict that it would continue to maintain its control of Congress in 1997 or win Mexico's presidential election in the year 2000.

Judicial Independence and the Court's New Judicial Review Powers

The establishment of judicial independence and the Supreme Court's new powers of judicial review were fundamental changes to Mexico's judicial branch. These changes, which were introduced and then fully implemented by the ruling party, served both the long-term and short-term interests of Zedillo and the weakening PRI.[23] As for judicial independence, the new appointment procedures for both justices and lower-level judges decreased future opportunities for partisan selection of judicial positions. In the long run, this would protect the PRI against the possibility of an opposition party coming to power and wielding influence over the Supreme Court and lower-level members of the judiciary. In the short term, the reform also benefited Zedillo by allowing him to rename the Supreme Court to his liking.

Institutional changes to judicial independence, it must be remembered, also imply potential costs for a ruling party. However, these costs were muted for Zedillo during his *sexenio*. As the PRI still controlled two-thirds of the Senate, Zedillo was able to have his Supreme Court nominees confirmed by the votes of his party acting alone. But he is likely to be the last Mexican president to enjoy such power. In addition, Zedillo had more say over the composition of the CFJ than will any future president. According to the rules, the president names only one appointee. However, as part of the reform package, Zedillo named all the members of the reconstituted Supreme Court. Because the Supreme Court's chief justice serves as the presiding member of the CFJ, Zedillo indirectly named another member of the council. Zedillo also wielded influence over the two appointees chosen by the PRI-controlled Senate. Hence, the real costs of increases in judicial independence in Mexico will be passed on to future politicians.

As for the court's new powers of judicial review, the extent of these new powers is particularly revealing as to the motivation behind the 1994 reform. The Supreme Court was not given full powers of judicial review. Rather, the high court's new constitutional controls were restricted to two specific areas—areas where the ruling party faced significant threats from its political rivals. Both the constitutional controversies and unconstitutional laws clauses would serve to protect the PRI where it had suffered losses of political power. While the PRI might not be able to prevent decisions and actions taken against its interests by opposition-controlled political offices, at least it could challenge these actions via an autonomous and empowered judiciary.

Specifically, constitutional controversies enabled the court to serve as an independent arbiter in disputes between government entities, a solution for a ruling party whose loss of power, particularly at the state and local level, had left it no longer capable of resolving issues quietly and unilaterally from behind closed doors. The unconstitutional laws clause allowed the PRI to use the court to check the arbitrary exercise of authority by executives and legislatures it could no longer control. Thus, via the use of the court's new constitutional control clauses, the PRI could protect itself against its current losses of political power at the state and local levels. Such protection would come in handy in the short term as further deterioration of the ruling party's political position in midterm elections during the Zedillo *sexenio* was likely. Furthermore, given the possibility that the PRI could lose the presidential election in 2000, the reformed court could provide a means of challenging Mexico's next ruling party.

Clearly, the PRI could have embarked on a reform granting the Mexican Supreme Court more extensive judicial review powers. For example, it could have granted the court expanded judicial review powers, adopted the principle of majority rule for declarations of unconstitutionality to take effect, or allowed for judicial review to be used against existing legislation rather than just within thirty days of the passage of a new law. But the PRI did not choose any of these courses of action. Instead, the court's two new constitutional control powers were specifically designed to counter the most salient threats posed by the increasing political power of the opposition. The party was not seeking a more powerful Supreme Court as an end in itself. Rather, the PRI's goal was to balance two competing desires: the desire to limit the court's ability to challenge the ruling party in the current period with the desire to use the court as protection from the opposition as the PRI was dethroned from its position. As an insurance policy, the ruling party was willing to accept costs in the immediate period (the costs associated with an independent judiciary ruling against the interests of the PRI during the Zedillo administration) as a security hedge against the possibility of paying higher costs later (the costs associated with an opposition party's coming to power and wielding unchecked authority contrary to the interests of the PRI).

Thus, while the decision by the ruling president and party to grant the Supreme Court the attributes of a constitutional court—and thereby check the power of the very government that initiated and approved judicial reform—appears illogical on the surface, it makes sense when regarded as an insurance policy sought by a weakening ruling party that could no longer guarantee its monopoly on political power. For the PRI, establishing judicial independence and granting the Supreme Court the power to invalidate laws and to decide boundary disputes over political power reduced the risks associated with the potential loss of the PRI's dominant political position. By December 1994 the PRI had already lost power and was likely to continue to do so; hence implementation immediately followed the initiation of judicial reform and did so in a way that upheld constitutional promises of judicial empowerment.

Additional Players in the Reform Decision

While Mexico's 1994 judicial reform was dictated from within the presidential palace, both domestic and international actors have been involved with certain aspects of it, although in general their role has been limited. Recognizing that judicial changes were imminent, several Supreme Court justices prepared their own judicial reform proposal and submitted it to the executive (Cossío-Díaz 1998b). According to José Ramón Cossío-Díaz, a constitutional specialist involved in the drafting of the court's judicial proposal, the court's reform would have emboldened it with extensive powers of judicial review (Cossío-Díaz 1998b).[24] The president's judicial reform initiative, however, was quite distinct from that of the Supreme Court—for example, firing the entire bench and granting the court much more narrowly defined powers of judicial review than those the court itself suggested. This demonstrates the court's limited influence on the 1994 reform package.

International financial institutions, as discussed in the introductory chapter of this book, have advocated judicial reform in Latin America as a way of promoting investor confidence in the region. But in the case of Mexico IFIs did not provide funds for judicial reform or link economic assistance to its undertaking. The World Bank did approve a $30 million loan to modernize Mexico's state (not federal) judicial services in 2004, but this loan was not tied to the 1994 reform enacted a decade earlier.[25] The most significant international assistance for judicial reform received by Mexico in the mid-1990s was small-scale funding from the United States Aid for International Development (USAID). This aid, however, addressed judicial training and not the empowerment of the Mexican Supreme Court (Perez 1998).[26]

Civil society organizations have also played a role in specific areas of justice reform in Mexico (for example, criminal and penal reforms), but not a major role in the restructuring of the judicial branch or the empowerment of the Supreme Court. According to Rafael Harel, vice president of Mexico's Commission on the Defense and Promotion of Human Rights, neither civil society nor human rights groups were influential or actively involved in the design of the 1994 reform (Harel 1998). Instead, the initiation and development of Mexico's judicial reforms was a presidential prerogative.

While the parameters of Mexico's judicial reform package were defined by the Zedillo administration, the president's party could not single-handedly approve constitutional changes to the judiciary. The Mexican constitution may be changed only with the approval of two-thirds of the representatives from each house of Congress. Although the PRI had two-thirds of the seats in the Senate, the party lacked this proportion in the Chamber of Deputies, and Zedillo was compelled to court the PAN in order to pass the judicial reform bill. As a result, the PAN was well placed at the bargaining table.

In exchange for its support of the PRI's reform proposal, the PAN was able to extract particular benefits from the PRI with respect to judicial reform and to modify the reform proposal to its advantage. With regard to the former, the reform established a more conservative Supreme Court, and the sympathies of at least four of the new justices, including the chief justice, lay with the PAN (Begné 1996). Also, the position of attorney general, the individual responsible for the implementation of judicial reform, was given to a member of the PAN.

Additionally, the PAN achieved several modifications to the PRI proposal, each of which favored the strengthening of the judiciary as a viable check on political power. First, Zedillo's original proposal granted the president the power to appoint two members of the Federal Judicial Council. During the bargaining in Congress, however, the number of appointees the president could name was lowered from two to one, thereby decreasing the executive's (in other words, the PRI's) weight in the council. Second, the president's proposed minimum of nine justices to allow a court ruling to have general effects was lowered to eight, thereby facilitating the ability of the court to declare laws unconstitutional.

Finally, the most significant modification of Zedillo's original proposal achieved by the PAN was the decrease in the number of legislators required to petition the Supreme Court under the reform's unconstitutionality of laws clause. Zedillo's original proposal had placed this requirement at 45 percent of the members of a legislature, but the reform bill was approved only after the percentage had been lowered to 33. The reduced percentage greatly enhanced the PAN's ability to challenge decisions made by the PRI. At that time the PAN held one-third of the seats in many northern state legislatures. It could also obtain this proportion in the Chamber of Deputies and in Mexico City's Legislative Assembly by joining with other opposition parties. Furthermore, with its strong prospects for the 1997 congressional elections, the PAN at that time was well placed to capitalize on the potential benefits of this change. Thus, for the PAN, the reform increased the number of institutional mechanisms available for challenging the PRI.

The most prominent political criticism of Mexico's 1994 reform proposal came from the PRD.[27] Since the PRD was also an opposition party, the argument of this study would predict that the PRD should support changes to increase judicial independence and improve the court's role in the separation of powers. Yet the PRD opposed the PRI-sponsored reform. This apparent paradox can be explained by examining the PRD's perspective more deeply. From the PRD's vantage point, the PRI's provision of limited judicial reform was intended to preserve the PRI's hold on power. This objective, however, undermined the public's perception of the need to engage in a more extensive overhaul of the judicial system, and therefore stymied attempts to undertake more profound political reforms (Penalosa 1996). Thus, as expected of an opposition party, the PRD did not oppose strengthening of the judiciary in principle, but it did oppose this particular reform package for not further empowering the Supreme Court. A PRI-PAN congressional coalition was nevertheless able to pass judicial reform without the support of the PRD, and the latter was therefore unable to obstruct or wield influence over Mexico's 1994 judicial reform.

Mexico's president, leader of the very same ruling party that oversaw the development of a Supreme Court that had refrained from challenging the party's authority over the course of nearly seven decades, deliberately undertook institutional reforms in 1994 to establish a judiciary with the potential to constrain the PRI's own political power. Zedillo initiated the reform process, defined the parameters of the debate, and specifically tailored the Supreme Court's two new powers of judicial review to protect the ruling party where it perceived itself to be the most vulnerable. Politicians from the ruling party, increasingly unable to control political outcomes at the state and local level and unsure whether they would maintain their dominance of the national government in the future, granted increased independence to the judiciary and the power of judicial review to the Supreme Court. In the Mexican case, the ruling party had the incentive to implement as well as to initiate judicial reform. The result has been a fundamental alteration in the balance of power between the executive and judicial branches and the creation of a Supreme Court able to enter the political fray.

Chapter Five

The Paradox of Latin America's Judicial Reforms: Lessons Learned

On the surface, Latin America's judicial reforms present a paradox: why would politicians enact institutional reforms that appear to limit their own political power? We can better answer this question by separating judicial reform into its two component stages, initiation and implementation. This book's investigation of judicial reform in Argentina, Peru, and Mexico reveals that although politicians were willing to initiate constitutional changes increasing judicial power, only under a particular set of circumstances were these leaders willing to follow through with the legislation necessary to make these changes a working reality. By examining variations in implementation of judicial reform, we can understand why some of Latin America's 1990s judicial reforms resulted in the establishment of more powerful judiciaries while others failed to do so.

While politicians in Argentina, Peru, and Mexico introduced similar constitutional reforms in the early 1990s, the results of these reforms varied greatly. In both Argentina and Peru these reforms were stymied during implementation, and the courts in these two countries remained unable to challenge political authority. It was not until 1999 and 2000, respectively, that presidents in Argentina and Peru finally relinquished control over the judicial branch. In Mexico, in contrast, meaningful implementation occurred shortly after initiation. As a result, the Mexican judiciary enjoyed new independence, and Mexico's Supreme Court proved able to check the exercise of political power. In all three cases, ruling parties sought the implementation of judiciary-strengthening reforms only once it appeared that they were losing their positions of political dominance.

Thus, to understand Latin America's recent judicial reforms, we have seen that it is essential to analyze the incentives faced by politicians at both the initiation and implementation stages. At initiation, the enactment of constitutional changes required either the support of two-thirds of the assembly authorized to rewrite the constitution (Congress or a constitutional convention), the support of the general public in a national referendum, or both. Both opposition political parties and voters called for the establishment of an empowered judiciary as a way to check potential abuses of power by the president and ruling party. In order to ensure the passage of proposed constitutional reforms, ruling parties in all three countries were forced to modify their initial reform proposals in ways that strengthened the judiciary.

In Argentina, Menem agreed to cede his influence on the Supreme Court and to establish an independent judicial council. In exchange he received the Radicals' support for a package of constitutional reforms that included his right to a second term. In Peru, Fujimori needed to obtain the support of the public to approve proposed constitutional reforms that included his right to re-election. Hence, counter to his initial proposals, Fujimori agreed to maintain the Constitutional Court and to allow an independent national magistrates council to select judges. In Mexico, the PRI needed the vote of the PAN to pass its judicial reform package in Congress. To obtain PAN support, the PRI was forced to modify its proposal in ways that facilitated the opposition's ability to make use of the Supreme Court's new powers of judicial review. Thus, in all three cases initiation resulted in the promulgation of dramatic constitutional revisions that appeared to empower domestic judicial institutions.

However, the political support required in each country to enact the necessary implementing legislation was not as stringent as the support required to initiate reforms. This had significant ramifications with respect to the ruling party's perceived costs—the possibility of judicial interference with the ruling party's exercise of authority—of reform. The ruling party incurs this cost only once the implementing legislation has been passed. But because enactment of congressional legislation required the approval of just a simple majority, the ruling party retained discretion over this second phase of reform. In effect, the costs of reform were minimized. Recalcitrant ruling parties could act to weaken, stall, or postpone entirely the previously agreed-upon increases in judicial power. In fact, this is what occurred in Argentina and Peru, where constitutional increases in judicial power were delayed (Argentina) or undermined (Peru) at the second stage of reform.

Given Argentina's and Peru's experiences with judicial reform, the question arises: if a government apparently has no real interest in later implementing judicial reform, why initiate it in the first place? I argue that political leaders were willing to engage in the initiation of judicial reform because it provided them with two specific and immediate benefits. The first benefit derived from satisfying the demands of international financial institutions. Initiating judicial reform was a way for governments to demonstrate progress on their IFI-sponsored structural adjustment programs. In return, that country was then rewarded with an IFI "stamp of approval," facilitating economic inflows from international agencies and investors. A second major benefit obtained from judicial reform was the use of judicial changes as a "bargaining chip" in which strengthening the judiciary was traded for some other institutional reform. In particular, presidents appeared willing to offer improvements to the national judiciary in exchange for the right to re-election, a constitutional reform that the ruling party could not otherwise obtain. Furthermore, the ruling party could enjoy both of judicial reform's benefits immediately at initiation. At the same time, as implementation would remain at the ruling party's discretion, the potential costs of reform to the ruling party at this stage were minimized. Thus, for the ruling party at initiation, the benefits of reform strongly outweighed the costs and the first stage of reform was easily achieved.

However, the ruling party's perceptions of judicial reform did not remain fixed between the initiation and implementation periods. In particular, the benefits to be obtained by the ruling party from continuing forward with judicial reform have decreasing returns. First, the IFIs have not offered additional economic assistance for progress on the implementation of judicial reform, nor have they imposed serious penalties for nonimplementation of such reform. Second, the benefits gained from a political trade in which judicial reforms are offered in exchange for some other institutional change are exhausted at the time the new constitution is enacted. For example, once the president has obtained the right to re-election in exchange for proclaiming increases in judicial power, the president may run for re-election and then enjoy a second term without implementing promised judicial reforms.

Thus, the benefits of judicial reform do not increase with implementation. Yet the costs of judicial reform, which remain only potential costs at initiation, become concrete realities if reform is implemented in the spirit of the new constitution. The effect of the convergence of decreasing benefits and increasing costs is the erosion of the will to carry through with the implementation of judicial reform. This pattern describes the experiences of Argentina and Peru.

Argentina's 1994 constitution granted increased independence to the Argentine judiciary. The opposition Radical Party, in exchange for its support of a new constitution allowing presidential re-election, demanded the replacement of several justices on the Supreme Court and the establishment of a national judicial council to guarantee the independence of the judicial branch. Argentina's then-president Carlos Menem agreed to these changes in order to obtain a particular benefit: the constitutional right to run for re-election. However, after his re-election and his party's triumph in Congress in 1995, Menem lost interest in implementing the agreed-upon judicial changes. From Menem's perspective, the benefits to be gained from judicial reform had been exhausted. Using his control of Congress, Menem delayed the creation of the council and failed to make the promised changes to the membership of the Supreme Court. For the next five years, the Radical Party continued to demand the enactment of the 1994 judicial reforms, albeit unsuccessfully.

In the Peruvian case, institutional changes included in that country's 1993 constitution greatly empowered the judicial branch. As in Argentina, these changes were part of a package of constitutional reforms that allowed the incumbent president to seek immediate re-election. In order to guarantee the popular support needed to approve the new constitution, Peru's then-president Alberto Fujimori agreed to the establishment of one of the most powerful judicial councils in the world as well as the continued existence of a constitutional court. However, after his 1995 re-election, Fujimori used his party's congressional majority to pass legislation eviscerating all judicial power. During the next two years, the Peruvian judiciary was placed under executive control, and both the National Magistrates Council and the Constitutional Court ceased to function in any meaningful way. Once Fujimori had exhausted the benefits to be obtained from the initiation of judicial reform, the costs of implementation were not offset by any additional gains. Instead, Fujimori effectively removed all potential judicial obstacles to the exercise of presidential power.

In contrast to the Argentine and Peruvian experiences, the Mexican government implemented its judicial reforms in accord with the constitutional changes just a few months after their December 1994 initiation. Given the costs of judicial reform, why would a ruling party cede power to the judicial branch? As we have seen, ruling parties facing the likely loss of political control have the incentive to seek increases in judicial power. In such a situation a ruling party may view judicial reform as a way to protect itself against the increasing power of its political rivals. An empowered judiciary may serve to check the ability of incoming politicians to alter the rules of the game in ways that undermine the interests of the outgoing ruling party. Thus, the implementation of meaningful judicial reforms is more likely to occur where these reforms serve the ruling party as a form of political insurance.

As for Mexico's 1994 reform, it fits the scenario of judicial reform as a political insurance policy. Politicians from the ruling PRI party, having suffered earlier losses at the local and state levels and increasingly unsure of their ability to retain control of the government at the national level, granted increased power to the Mexican judiciary. The court's new powers of judicial review were specifically tailored to protect the PRI against threats posed by the increasing power of opposition parties. The PRI could obtain the benefits from judicial reform—political protection—only once it was implemented. Thus, the ruling party had the incentive both to initiate and implement judicial reform. The result of Mexico's 1994 judicial reform has been the development of a judicial branch capable of successfully challenging governmental authority.

On the other hand, presidents in Argentina and Peru, who were originally unwilling to accept agreed-upon reductions in executive discretion that would have resulted from the creation of more powerful judiciaries, did eventually enact these reforms. But they did not do so until it appeared likely that they would be leaving office, five and seven years respectively after their country's original constitutional reforms. In Argentina, the National Judicial Council was not enabled to sit until early 1999, at a time when it appeared that the Argentine ruling party would lose both the presidential and congressional elections later that year. In Peru, it was only after Fujimori was forced to resign, following a September 2000 corruption scandal, that the president instructed Congress to revoke executive control over the judicial branch. Although they had been unwilling to allow judicial constraints upon their own executive action, given their loss of political power these two presidents had the incentive to empower the judiciary as a check on future leaders.

These three Latin American case studies suggest several lessons for other countries undergoing judicial reform in the developing world. First, the cases reveal why the transition to a market economy cannot explain the divergent outcomes of Latin America's recent round of judicial reforms: economic concerns *are not sufficient* to persuade political leaders to follow through with the implementation of meaningful judicial reform. While Latin American political leaders have repeatedly recognized judicial reform as a necessary complement to economic restructuring, and while they have also been willing to acknowledge the IFIs' call for judicial independence, economic concerns have proved expendable where they conflict with the political interests of those in power. The economic benefits to be obtained from following through with judicial reform are not enough to outweigh the resulting political costs. External agents, whether multilateral agencies, foreign governments, or nongovernmental institutions, should understand that a government's economic concerns alone will not produce effective judicial reform. Additionally, IFIs must recognize that linking economic assistance to judicial reform will be ineffectual without imposing real penalties for failed performance.

Second, the benchmark for evaluating a country's progress on judicial reform should be its implementation, not its initiation. Constitutional increases in judicial power may be undermined or postponed by legislation that often remains in the hands of the ruling party. Thus, politicians who seek to strengthen the judicial branch should push to specify the details of the new judicial institutions in the revised constitution.

They will also need to find creative ways to lock in these changes on a fixed timeline, perhaps by agreeing that certain institutional changes come on-line simultaneously or not at all.

Third, powerful postreform judiciaries may not emerge in the more democratic of the developing countries, but rather in those countries where the reform serves the ruling party as insurance against future political uncertainty. For example, a casual observer might have expected that the most extensive reforms would occur in the most democratic country. At the time when each country's reform occurred, Argentina had a stable and well-functioning democracy. Peru was a formal democracy, in that it had free and competitive elections, but it was dominated by an excessively strong executive. Mexico was a one-party-dominant system featuring a ruling party that had held power for nearly seventy years and would have been considered the least democratic of the three. Thus, of these three cases, the most progress toward a powerful judiciary should have occurred in Argentina. Yet it was in Mexico that judicial reform went the furthest in establishing a judicial branch capable of checking government authority. Successful judicial reform appears to be linked to politicians seeking to protect themselves; however, it appears that the long-term consequences of such political insurance may be an autonomous judiciary able to serve as a true check on political power.

Finally, judicial reforms in Argentina, Peru, and Mexico were fully enacted only once the ruling party believed it was likely to lose its position of political dominance. These cases suggest that as the probability of retaining control over political power declines, the likelihood of full implementation of judicial reform increases. Furthermore, judicial reform is an example of a more general phenomenon—namely, the purposeful dispersion of political power by those who otherwise hold a monopoly. This book implies that democracy-building institutional reform and the likelihood of retaining office should share an inverse relationship. As the probability of retaining control over political office decreases, the motivation for carrying out institutional reform to place constraints on political power increases.

In the last decade, judicial reform has become a buzzword in Latin America. Such reform is tightly interwoven with the process of democratization that is occurring throughout the region. An independent judiciary, capable of enforcing limits on the exercise of government authority, is necessary for the proper functioning of a political system based on the separation of powers. It is also crucial for ensuring the development of the rule of law, the protection of individual liberties, and the prevention of human rights abuses. Our knowledge of the type of reforms that lead to an empowered judiciary is well developed. This book hopes to shed light on the circumstances under which we find the existence of the political will necessary to follow through with the implementation of judiciary-strengthening reforms.

Notes

Introduction

1. While this book is concerned primarily with Latin America, the challenge of establishing judiciaries capable of placing checks on authority holds true for much of the developing world.

2. For classic pieces on Latin American judiciaries, see Clagett 1952; Johnson 1976; Verner 1984; and Rosenn 1987.

3. For more on the rule of law see Dicey 1939. The definition of democracy used here comes from Diamond, Linz, and Lipset 1989, xvi, and includes "meaningful and extensive competition among individuals and organized groups (especially political parties) for all effective positions of government power, at regular intervals and excluding the use of force; a highly inclusive level of political participation in the selection of leaders and policies, at least through regular and fair elections, such that no major (adult) social group is excluded; and a level of civil and political liberties— freedom of expression, freedom of the press, freedom to form and join organizations—sufficient to ensure the integrity of political competition and participation."

4. Landes and Posner define an independent judiciary as "one that doesn't make decisions on the basis of the sorts of political factors (electoral strength of people affected by a decision) that would influence, control the decision were it to be made by a legislature" (1975, 895). For Iaryczower, Spiller, and Tomassi, judicial independence is the extent to which justices can reflect their preferences in their decisions without facing retaliation measures by Congress or the president (2002, 699). Fiss's discussion of judicial independence is three-pronged and relies on party detachment (judges are impartial to litigants before them), individual autonomy (judges are not controlled by other judges in the judicial hierarchy), and political insulary

(judges are free from control by other government institutions) (1993, 55–56). According to Christopher Larkins's definition, "Judicial independence refers to the existence of judges who are not manipulated for political gain, impartial toward the parties in the dispute, part of a judicial branch which has the power as an institution to regulate the legality of government behavior, enact neutral justice, and determine significant legal and constitutional values" (1996, 611).

5. In Latin America, it is often stated that courts have the power of *revision judicial* (judicial review) because a law may be declared unconstitutional for an individual in a particular case—although the law remains in force for the rest of the population. Thus, scholars familiar with the understanding of the term *judicial review* as it is used in the English language should be aware of the different meaning in Spanish.

6. Civil law systems developed in eighteenth-century postrevolutionary France, at a time when government leaders were wary of the power of judges. Hence, civil law judges could neither make nor unmake laws, and this was achieved by limiting the effect of their rulings to the litigants involved. Under common law, judges' decisions are said to have "general effects," meaning that a court's ruling applies to all citizens and political entities within the country, not just those individuals involved in the case. The extended effect of judicial decisions under common law allows for the total invalidation of a law; the law may no longer be applied and is therefore null and void. See Merryman 1985 for a good overview of civil law systems.

7. Austrian jurist Hans Kelsen first proposed the idea of a constitutional court as a source of constitutional control in *General Theory of Law and State*. According to Kelsen, "The application of the constitutional rules concerning legislation can be effectively guaranteed only if an organ other than the legislative body is entrusted with the task of testing whether a law is constitutional, and of annulling it if—according to the opinion of the organ—it is 'unconstitutional'" (Kelsen 1945, 157). In Continental Europe today, the role of these courts is not only to declare legislation found unconstitutional to be null and void, but also to confer legitimacy upon laws they find constitutional (European Commission for Democracy Through Law 1994, 21). The creation of such courts in the developing world has lagged behind its European counterparts, but the trend of increasing the judiciary's role as a source of constitutional control in non-European civil law countries is growing (Merryman 1985).

8. For example, when Peru's Constitutional Court ruled in 1996 that the Peruvian president did not have a right to seek a third (and constitution-

ally illegal) term, the president had Congress fire three of the court's justices. In addition, Fujimori intimidated Justice Delia Revoredo Mur (one of the fired justices) by filing an arrest warrant for her husband and then establishing a special temporary court with which to try him, thereby forcing Mr. Mur to flee to Costa Rica.

9. Besides the countries under study here, constitutional judicial reforms were passed in Colombia (1991), Bolivia (1994), Ecuador (1998), and Venezuela (1999), among others.

10. For example, Colombia, Peru, and Venezuela have constitutional tribunals that are separate from their supreme courts; Costa Rica created a special (and quite active) constitutional chamber within its traditional Supreme Court; and the Mexican Supreme Court was formally granted judicial review powers in specific circumstances.

11. For a detailed discussion of Latin American judicial councils, see Hammergren 2002b.

12. Other National Judicial Council functions may include control over the judicial budget; territorial division of the country into judgeships; establishment of internal regulations, such as working conditions and business hours; collection of data to monitor and evaluate the quality of judicial services; and publication of judicial decisions.

13. The inclusion of government appointments on council compositions has sparked controversy, but such councils may still foster judicial independence as long as the overall balance of the members allows for autonomous decision making.

14. According to Pásara, in spite of the "general absence of organizations representing civil society" (2003, 17) in judicial reform, NGOs have successfully promoted changes in the areas of human rights, reform of the penal process, and public interest litigation (24–28).

15. In Argentina, Carlos Zamorano, co-president of the Argentine League for the Rights of Man, stated that the primary judicial concern of human rights groups there had been trials of human rights violators, not structural reforms. In addition, with respect to Argentina's 1994 constitutional revisions, Zamorano noted that while human rights organizations had pushed for the explicit inclusion of individual and group rights in the new constitution, they had not been involved in the political pact that reformed the judicial branch (Zamorano 1999). As for Peru, Carlos Basombrio, director of the Institute for Legal Defense, stated that human rights groups did not play a significant role in the restructuring of judicial institutions in the 1993 constitutional reform (Basombrio 1997a). Rafael Harel, vice

president of Mexico's Commission on the Defense and Promotion of Human Rights in 1998, stated that neither civil society nor human rights groups were influential or actively involved in the design of Mexico's 1994 judicial reform (Harel 1998). However, according to World Bank judicial sector specialist for Latin America Linn Hammergren, human rights were part of the push for structural judicial reforms in Central America in the 1980s. Unlike judicial reform in the larger countries of Latin America, judicial reform in Honduras, Guatemala, and El Salvador was part of peace settlements funded by international donors, and these external donors were concerned with human rights (Hammergren 1999).

16. The Supreme Court of Mexico declared unconstitutional a law intended to guarantee the PRI a majority of seats (even if the PRI obtained only a plurality of the popular vote) in the Quintana Roo state legislature; see *Unconstitutional Laws 6/98*, September 23, 1998. For a detailed discussion of this case, see Finkel 2003.

Chapter One
Explaining Latin America's Recent Judicial Reforms

1. The Law and Development Movement of the 1960s and 1970s, a period of concern with legal institutions and economic growth in Latin America, resulted in the funding of legal reform by development agencies throughout the region. However, the movement ultimately failed due to weak theory, low in-country participation, and the false belief that U.S. legal institutions could be readily installed abroad (Messick 1999, 125–26; Ginsburg 2000, 829–30).

2. Unlike neoclassical economic theory, in which institutions necessary for economic growth are assumed to exist and to operate perfectly (Joskow 2004), NIE postulates that (1) institutions matter and (2) they are susceptible to analysis by economic tools (Matthews 1986, 908). NIE owes a legacy to Ronald Coase's pioneering work on transaction costs (the costs of specifying what is being exchanged and then monitoring and enforcing that agreement *ex post*) and the relationship between the costs of exchange and economic productivity (1937, 1960).

3. For example, in addition to the research on institutions highlighted here, NIE also examines informal norms and traditions at the macrolevel, "rules of play" of firms, hybrids and bureaucracies, and resource allocation and employment at the microlevel (Williamson 2000).

4. North and Weingast's classic piece on seventeenth-century England demonstrates how the development of constitutional arrangements allowing the government to make credible commitments to uphold property rights—in contrast to its earlier pattern of royal prerogatives and confiscatory behavior—resulted in the remarkable performance of the English economy in the period following the 1688/89 Glorious Revolution (1989).

5. NIE, while it overlaps with the field of law and economics in its concern with property rights and contract law, is distinct from the latter. Law and economics, also known as economic analysis of law (EAL), concerns itself with (1) the effect of law and legal institutions on individual behavior, and (2) the search for legal rules that are socially desirable (Kaplow and Shavell 1999). Major contributions to EAL have been Coase's work on externalities and legal liabilities (1960), Becker's study on crime and law enforcement (1968), Calabresi's research on accident law (1970), and Posner's textbook on EAL (1972) and his founding of the *Journal of Legal Studies* (Kaplow and Shavell 1999, 3).

6. The ideas of Douglass North began to circulate in Latin American academia in the early 1990s, and their dissemination increased dramatically following North's receipt of the Nobel Prize in economics in 1993 (Cárdenas 1997).

7. The specific projects supported by the World Bank are strengthening the judicial branch (improving the independence of judges and judicial control over their own finances), promoting celerity in the processing of cases, improving judicial infrastructure and technology, developing alternative dispute resolution mechanisms, and professionalizing the bench and the bar (Messick 2002).

8. As of 2002, the World Bank alone had extended $121.9 million in judicial reform projects to seven countries in Latin America (Messick 2002). More broadly, the World Bank, the Inter-American Development Bank, and the Asian Development Bank have extended over $800 million in judicial reform loans to the developing world (Messick 2002). IFIs supply an estimated three-fourths of all funds used for judicial reform in the developing world, with the World Bank estimated to be supplying about half of the total funds.

9. As of the mid-1990s, the Inter-American Development Bank was the only international agency to provide Mexico with funds for judicial reform, but this was only a minimal amount to sponsor a small arbitration project. On July 1, 2004, the World Bank approved a US$30 million loan to improve state (not federal) judicial services in Mexico. USAID is currently seeking to

sponsor in Mexico a US$5 million justice initiative concentrating on penal reform, legal training, and access to justice for marginalized communities.

10. In 1998 the Inter-American Development Bank approved a $10.5 million loan agreement for Argentina to modernize its judicial sector (Inter-American Development Bank 2006). That same year, the World Bank approved a US$5 million dollar loan to support the development of twelve first-instance model courts (Messick 2002).

11. Mancur Olson explicitly notes the link between the protection of economic and political rights, "conditions needed to have the individual rights needed for economic development are exactly the same conditions that are needed to have a lasting democracy" (Olson 1993, 572).

12. Ramseyer's 1994 article examines judicial politics in the United States, modern Japan, and imperial Japan. Both of Ramseyer's conditions hold true for the United States over time, and this has lead to the independence of American judges. As for imperial Japan, the belief that continued elections were unlikely undermined incentives to allow judicial independence. In postwar Japanese politics, Liberal Democratic Party (LDP) dominance and the LDP's belief in the likelihood of continued electoral victory determined its preference for nonindependent judges. These ideas are further detailed in Ramseyer and Rasmusen 2003.

13. According to Hirschl, the creation of Israel's 1992 Basic Law (a document that fulfills the same function as a Bill of Rights) was the result of the secular Ashkenazi ruling group's fearing the inroads of new political interests (lower income non-Ashkenazi Jews, Israeli-Arabs, and religious parties), and so it sought to transfer political struggles to the Israeli Supreme Court, as these justices were more in line with the secular, neoliberal philosophy of the Ashkenazi leaders who had traditionally dominated Israeli politics.

14. Rebecca Bill-Chavez, in a well-researched and elegant analysis of judicial structures in two provinces in Argentina, also argues that party fragmentation is crucial for the development of an autonomous judiciary (2003).

15. Besides the two major payoffs, the initiation of judicial reform also has other possible minor benefits for the ruling party. These include increases in private investment, a positive international image, and favorable domestic public opinion. The payoff from these rewards is minimized, however, because their value is less certain and because they have less effect on short-term political survival. For example, by bolstering investor confidence, judicial reform could lead to increased private investment. Yet investment levels might not be affected in the current period as it would take time

for investors to develop trust in the newly reformed judiciary. Second, although initiation could be used to curry favor with international human rights groups or foreign governments, this might not lead to tangible benefits for the ruling party. Third, judicial reform could be a way for a political party to sell itself as the party of the "rule of law," but it is unclear how strongly this would affect levels of support as voters have been hesitant to accept these reforms at face value.

16. In fact, the opposition can only enjoy the benefits of judicial reform once the initiated reforms are implemented.

17. Only in cases of egregious violations of judicial independence have judicial reform loans been terminated. And yet even in those extreme cases, the disbursement of all other IFI development assistance was not affected. Thus, the payoff from the IFIs, a stamp of approval, is enjoyed at the initiation of judicial reform, and it appears not to be affected regardless of what happens during the implementation phase.

Chapter Two
Judicial Reform in Argentina in the 1990s

An earlier version of this chapter was published as "Judicial Reform in Argentina in the 1990s: How Electoral Incentives Shape Institutional Change," *Latin American Research Review* 39, no. 3 (October 2004): 56-80.

1. Molinelli presents a more favorable view of Argentine judicial power, arguing that the court has increased its autonomy over time and has been willing to reverse the government on important cases (1999).

2. Helmke demonstrates that antigovernment rulings cluster at the end of weak governments, both democratic and nondemocratic; Iaryczower, Spiller, and Tomassi show that judicial independence cannot be measured by the reversal of government decisions alone; and Bill-Chavez argues that divided government is key for the development of judicial autonomy.

3. The court did not just abrogate law (suspend its application), but declared it null and void (having no legal consequence). Its ruling further declared that laws passed by de facto regimes carry less constitutional merit than those passed by democratically elected governments. The decision was seen as a significant victory for the human rights community. However, the ruling was later rescinded in the 1990s in a case heard by Menem's enlarged court. See Zamorano 1999.

4. For more on these trials see Rabossi 1993.

5. The proposal granted civilian courts ultimate authority over the trial of military officials who perpetrated human rights violations between 1976 and 1983. Judicial proceedings would begin in military tribunals, and these tribunals were to report their progress to a federal court of appeals within six months. At that time, the civilian appeals court could decide whether to assume jurisdiction or to grant an extension to the military tribunal.

6. The Radicals were Gemaro Carrio (Alfonsín faction), Jose Severo Caballero (Cordoba faction), Augusto Belluscio (Alvearista faction); the Socialist was Carlos Fayt; and the traditional Peronist, Enrique Petracchi.

7. The Final Stop Law gave the courts a forty-day deadline to complete all trials of military personnel. After that date, no new trials could be opened and all pending trials would be considered closed even if they had not been resolved. The Law of Due Obedience stated that lower-level officers could not be held accountable for human rights violations committed while carrying out the orders of their superiors. For more on these laws, see Acuna and Smulovitz 1995.

8. The Peronists preferred the higher number in order to satisfy various factions within their party; see "Elevarían a Nueve los Miembros de la Corte," *La Nación,* January 4, 1988, 1.

9. The document makes no mention of re-election. However, the individual reform proposals put forth that same year show important differences on this issue, with the Radicals opposing re-election and the Peronists favoring it for all political offices.

10. Menem issued a total of 244 decree laws in his first three years in office, more than all of Argentina's other constitutionally elected presidents combined. Alfonsín issued only twenty-two in his entire six-year tenure (Larkins 1998, 425).

11. According to Eduardo Grana, a judge and National Judicial Council member, "Menem knew that sectors in society would go to the High Court in opposition to its economic reform program." See Grana 1999.

12. In a television interview, Menem justified his attempt to pack his country's Supreme Court, stating, "Why should I be the only president in 50 years who hasn't had his own Court?" (Larkins 1998, 428).

13. Allegedly, custodial staff were instructed to sit in the benches for the hand vote (Verbitsky 1993, 49–51).

14. Larkins 1998, 6. Citing an April 27, 1993, interview.

15. Comparing Menem's court to Alfonsín's, Larkins writes, "The [post-1990] Court has set solid precedents on the extent of the President's decree authority, civil-military and federal-provincial relations, the validity of de-

crees issued by de facto governments, and the validity of government contracts. The key difference, of course, is that on virtually all of these occasions, the Supreme Court's decisions have either directly supported or strongly favored the President's policies" (1998, 431–32).

16. The Minority Office of the Chamber of Deputies, controlled by the Radicals, issued a statement against amending the constitution, claiming that "to sponsor reform only to assure presidential reelection would constitute a grave error . . . it would signify confusing reform with a personal project" (*Después de la Reforma de la Constitución* n.d., 21).

17. It may have been possible to achieve two-thirds of the total members by striking bargains with small provincial parties that had representation in the chamber, but the Peronists could not guarantee that they could obtain these crucial votes. In addition, according to Catalina Smulovitz, Menem preferred to have the Radicals support the reform to increase the legitimacy of his re-election aspirations. See Smulovitz 1999.

18. The Peronists also sought to obtain constitutional authorization for the executive to issue decrees.

19. The declaratory law also specified issues, such as popular referendums, indigenous identity, municipal autonomy, and environmental protection, among others, which could be individually introduced at the convention.

20. Seventeen other parties participated in the constitutional assembly but could exert little influence.

21. Justices Barra and Carvagno Martinez announced their immediate resignations; Justice Levene declared he would resign in February. The Radicals had demanded the resignations of Barra and Carvagno Martinez, considering them to be the most militant in their sympathies for the government.

22. The Radical Bossert would replace Carvagno, the Peronist Lopez would replace Barra, and the Radical Mansatta would replace Levene. See Grana 1999.

23. According to Eduardo Barcesat, a Constitutional Assembly opposition representative, the incoming Peronist justice Guillermo Lopez had a tight connection with Menem. But since the Radicals believed they would still have a majority on the court, they accepted Lopez's appointment. See Barcesat 1999.

24. The reform also placed a limit on the age of justices. From this point on, justices had to be under the age of seventy-five to be appointed, and all justices on the court who were over seventy-five would have to be ratified by the Senate every five years.

25. See Chavez for a detailed discussion of Argentina's Judicial Council (2004).

26. According to Arturo Pellet Lastra, Menem did not rely on outright coercion to control court decision making; rather "his influence over the court operated on a system of pressures, favors, and friendships." See Pellet Lastra 1999.

27. Speaking off the record to Argentine journalist Adrian Ventura, Supreme Court Chief Justice Nazareno, alluding to any possible future corruption scandals implicating Menem once he was no longer in office, stated, "Do you think Menem will get rid of the judges who will save him?" See Ventura 1999.

28. Meanwhile, members of Menem's Supreme Court were forcefully opposing the council's creation. Chief Justice Nazareno called the creation of the council an attempt to "behead" the Supreme Court (*La Nación* 1996a, 8). Nazareno and the court's vice chief justice met with Menem at the Casa Rosada to express their "profound concern" over the creation of the council. In particular, they opposed the council's usurpation of two of their key functions, oversight of the judicial budget and control over judicial discipline, and they asked the president to modify the Senate's proposal to return these functions to the Court (*Clarín* 1996a, 3). Justice Vazquez, always ready to defend government interests, repeatedly criticized the council as "a step backwards for democracy" (Boschi 1996, 6).

29. Quiroga Lavie stated, "The World Bank and other international financial organizations were making statements here [in Argentina] for some time about the needs of a market economy and judicial security, and this was understood and recognized by high political officials in Argentina." See Quiroga Lavie 1999.

30. Examples include: William Davies's *Informe Sobre los Problemas del Sector Judicial de la Argentina,* in December 1992; a USAID–Argentine Law Foundation joint report produced in February 1993; Rafael Bielsa's *Transformacion del Derecho en Justicia,* published in 1993; and "Economic Transformation and Judicial Security," working paper presented by the Research Institute for the New State (University of Belgrano) at its 1994 seminar series.

31. The speech, given at a three-day colloquium sponsored by the Institute for Entrepreneurial Development in Argentina, was attended by President Menem, Argentine congressmen, international economists, and representatives from more than two hundred of Argentina's most important businesses. Instituto para el Desarollo de Empresarios en la Argentina, "La Empresa ante el Cambio," colloquium held in Buenos Aires, September

13–16, 1992. Other examples of public statements commenting on the need to strengthen the judiciary to induce investment abound. For example, in 1990 the Chamber of Deputies' Justice Committee chair asked, "What foreign investor would have confidence in a country that does not assure the payment of a promissory note?" (*La Nación* 1990b, 1). Furthermore, the U.S. ambassador, addressing the Argentine Supreme Court in late 1993, stated, "Many North American companies have expressed an interest in seeing greater judicial security within the country in order to invest" (Verbitsky 1993, 17). Additionally, according to law professor Roberto Saaba, domestic entrepreneurs were equally concerned with the "pliability" and inefficiency of the Argentine judiciary. See Saaba 1999.

32. Frepaso itself was an alliance of smaller center-left parties. With a strong showing in the 1995 presidential and legislative elections, it had been challenging the Radicals for the position of dominant opposition party in Argentina.

33. Law 24.939, published January 2, 1998.

34. One of the academic representatives was the last to be chosen. This representative was to be selected by the deans of thirty-two national law schools, and many of these were smaller universities that depended on the government for their budget (Ventura 1998b).

35. The council was considering a six-month selection procedure to fill new appointments, with examinations beginning in May and appointments made no earlier than November. Quiroga Lavie 1999.

36. Centro de Estudios de Opinión Publica, November 1, 1998.

37. The council did cause the president consternation during the short period that they coexisted. For example, Menem yearned to fill a vacant spot on the Federal Electoral Tribunal, which would be the first-instance court for any "re-re-election" trials pertaining to Menem's desired third presidential bid. Thus, Menem attempted to try a new strategy of transferring Menem-friendly judges from unimportant posts to politically valuable judgeships. Menem's goal was to place a Peronist judge in the empty seat on the Federal Electoral Tribunal. The new judge, the brother of Menem's interior minister, had already been picked out. The National Judicial Council, however, quickly killed the executive's proposal to grant himself the power to transfer judges.

38. Specifically, the Acuerdo stipulated only that the new constitution "ensure judicial independence by substantially modifying the method of designating judges so as to guarantee that 'moral fitness' be the primary reason for their selection." *Después de la Reforma de la Constitución* n.d., 22.

39. García-Lema 1994, 214–18. The Radical-Peronist judicial constitutional commission began to work with the report immediately following the signing of the Acuerdo, and this was an important source behind the creation of Argentina's Judicial Council (Ventura 1998a, 183).

40. See Smulovitz 1995, 79–81.

41. The Radicals did not formalize membership of the council at the convention. But given their assumed control over the Supreme Court, they had less to fear from lower-level judges.

Chapter Three
Judicial Reform in Peru in the 1990s

1. *Fiscales,* or state prosecutors, are members of the Public Ministry. They conduct preliminary investigations of charges of state abuse of authority, make recommendations about whether there exists enough evidence to go to trial, and undertake criminal investigations. The structure of the Public Ministry parallels that of the judicial branch, with the Supreme Junta of Fiscales on a par with the Supreme Court, and first- and second-instance *fiscales* serving as the counterparts to first- and second-instance judges. In Peru the word *magistrates* refers to both judges and *fiscales.*

2. The initial naming of the Constitutional Court via staggered selection allowed the Peruvian presidents of the 1980–85 and 1985–90 administrations to wield great influence over the membership of the court. By Fujimori's presidency, however, the executive could no longer wield such influence, showing that the system might have been effective if it had been allowed to develop.

3. Of the Peruvians who had used the judiciary, 80 percent claimed that they did not trust it and were dissatisfied with the service they received (De Belaunde 1991, 39).

4. Fujimori's August 24 speech, cited in Abad Yupanqui and Garcés Peralta 1993, 99.

5. The National Magistrates Council proposed seven candidates to fill these newly created positions on the Supreme Court. However, Fujimori ignored their candidates in favor of his own hand-picked appointments.

6. Shining Path was then Peru's most notorious terrorist group. The Supreme Court's decision to release its leader, Abimael Guzman, on the grounds of insufficient evidence further weakened the status of the court in the eyes of the general public.

7. Fujimori's minister of transport, in an attempt to circumvent compliance with the decision, declared the ruling "inapplicable" (Abad Yupanqui and Garcés Peralta 1993, 137).

8. Montesinos, after having played a key role in Fujimori's campaign, later became head of Peru's emboldened Servicio de Inteligencia Nacional (Schmidt 2000), where he oversaw a web of corruption and human rights violations. Montesinos was also the primary figure orchestrating "influence trafficking" within the judiciary during the Fujimori years (Rospigliosi 1997).

9. According to public opinion polls, 75 percent of the population supported the *auto-golpe. New York Times*, April 9, 1992, 2.

10. For example, polls conducted in four major cities showed that those cities would vote against the new constitution by 57.2 percent, 45.7 percent, 50.2 percent, and 62 percent, respectively. The vote in favor for each city was only 10.4 percent, 19.4 percent, 15.2 percent, and 11.3 percent. *Caretas* 1993, 16.

11. Another innovative development was the creation of an ombudsman's office (Defensoría del Pueblo), responsible for the protection and promotion of human rights, in the new constitution. This provision was offered as a counterweight to the 1993 constitution's authorization of increased power to the military. Article 143 of the new constitution allowed military courts to try civilian suspects accused of terrorism or "treason against the state." Previously, jurisdiction of Peru's military tribunals was limited to the armed forces. Second, Article 173 authorized military tribunals to impose the death penalty for persons convicted of terrorism or "treason against the state" despite Peru's legal tradition that considered capital punishment to be unconstitutional. According to Carlos Basombrio, president of the human rights group Institute for Legal Defense in 1997, even with the inclusion of an ombudsman's office in the new constitution, human rights groups voiced strong criticism of the new constitution for its increases in military prerogatives (Basombrio 1997b).

12. In Spanish these are known as *jueces de paz*, and in Peru today there are about four thousand of them operating in rural and marginalized areas. In contrast to most other judges in Peru, the *jueces de paz* have been widely respected and have polled strong approval ratings in the communities they serve. See Lovatón Palacios and Ardito Vega 2002.

13. For example, the U.S. Department of State Report analysis of Peru's 1993 constitution concluded that it "granted more power to the executive than prior constitutions, but at the same time it gave increased independence to the Judicial Branch" (Comisión Andino de Juristas 1994, 56).

14. However, the Constitutional Court was left vacant.

15. The term used for ratified judges in Peru is *titulado*, or "titled," but here I refer to them as "tenured," which better conveys the meaning of the term in English.

16. Although limited in number, these few tenured superior-level magistrates proved willing to rule against the government. For example, in 1992 allegations surfaced implicating the military in the kidnapping and murder of nine students and their professor in the infamous human rights cases, *La Cantuta*. A provisional *fiscal*, William Paco Castillo, ruled that there was not sufficient reason to proceed with an investigation. The case was reopened when new evidence surfaced in 1993, and this time a tenured *fiscal*, Victor Cubas, was on "watch" and was therefore assigned to the case. Cubas, although threatened by the government and the military, filed a report stating that enough evidence existed to accuse the military and bring the case to trial. The military officials involved were found guilty in a court presided over by a tenured magistrate and sentenced to jail in 1994. After serving only a few months, they were pardoned by the passage of the government's 1995 amnesty law. As for William Paco Castillo, the Executive Commission later promoted him to the position of *fiscal* superior (Jimenez 1998). For more on *La Cantuta*, see Cubas 1998.

17. Rulings pertaining to the protection of individual rights (*habeas corpus* or *amparo*), however, would require the agreement of only a simple majority of justices (four out of seven).

18. Fujimori obtained 64 percent of the vote, and his party obtained a 67-seat majority in the 120-member Congress (Conaghan 1998, 5).

19. The chief justice at the time, Moises Pantoja, had been on the Supreme Court prior to the coup. He was one of four justices whom Fujimori renamed to the court after the *auto-golpe*. Although Pantoja was the youngest justice on the eighteen-member court in 1994, he was selected as its chief justice. Francisco Eguiguren, then head of the Judicial Academy, stated that Fujimori had wanted Pantoja to be made the chief justice because "Pantoja was the most submissive" (Eguiguren 1997). However, many Peruvian legal experts, even though they believed that the judiciary should not be administered from outside the judicial branch, gave this first Executive Commission good marks. In fact, according to legal specialist Jose Ugaz, Dellepiane's commission managed to "break the inertia" and introduced some positive administrative changes (Ugaz 1997).

20. In all, Law 26623 suspended twenty-one articles of the October 1994 Organic Law of Judiciary.

21. A similar fate was also suffered by the Public Ministry, which was likewise placed under a separate executive commission until December 1998.

22. This led to fierce battles between the academy and the Magistrates Council over the judicial preparatory courses. The council wanted the courses to begin in May of 1997, to be of short duration, and to begin with superior-level magistrates in Lima. The Executive Commission was hoping to make the courses last for one year. In the end, the academy started the classes in July for justices of the peace, and their duration was six months. This was intended to prevent the council from tenuring the more politically important posts of first- and second-instance magistrates (Montoya Anguerry 1997).

23. For example, the Executive Commission initiated a system of financial bonuses to be distributed to judges at the end of the year. The commission would determine the amount of each individual's bonus, a sum that could equal the amount of a judge's annual salary (Ugaz 1997).

24. Interestingly, along with the passage of Law 26623 came a significant inflow of funds to the judicial branch from the government. According to Francisco Eguiguren, then head of the Judicial Academy, between June and November 1996 Dellepiane's commission spent between $20 and $25 million. Eguiguren stated that while the distribution of these funds was "hardly transparent," much of it was used to pay for the government's program of early retirement for judicial bureaucrats, with the rest spent on infrastructure, administration, and judicial career development (Eguiguren 1997).

25. Of note, the few judges who were willing to make decisions against the military for human rights violations were tenured. Examples include a ruling favoring Leonora de la Rosa, who had been tortured by the National Intelligence Service for revealing information about military human rights violations, and a decision favoring General Robles, a military official who had provided information on the location of the graves of victims murdered by the military in the 1992 *La Cantuta* case.

26. In all, the council ratified 258 superior-level judges and *fiscales*, as well as two supreme *fiscales* (Montoya Anguerry 2001).

27. Law 26738.

28. For example, by mid-1997 the commission had appointed sixteen provisional justices to the Supreme Court. Of the original eighteen justices tenured by the Tribunal of Honor, two were no longer on the court. Thus by June 1997 the court was evenly divided between provisional and tenured justices. Similarly, the Supreme Junta was also packed with provisional *fiscales*.

29. Carlos Torres y Torres Lara quoted in *El Comercio* 1997b, A4.

30. *El Comercio* 1997c, A2.

31. *La Republica* 1997, 1.

32. The law enabled Fujimori to control Peru's National Electoral Jury, the body that he had devised to determine whether the president had a right to a third consecutive term. The five-member jury was composed of one representative from the Supreme Court, one from the Supreme Junta of Fiscales, one from the national law schools, one from the private law schools, and one from the national bar association. The president could not control the votes of the representatives from the private law schools and the bar association, and correctly predicted that they would vote against him. By adding provisional members to the Supreme Court and the Supreme Junta, and then giving these members the right to vote on decisions taken by their institution and also to serve on the jury, Fujimori ensured that these two representatives would support his right to a third term. In addition, Fujimori had earlier "reorganized" the national law schools and was thus guaranteed the favorable vote of their representative. The jury later voted three to two to allow Fujimori to seek another presidential term (Cubas 1997a).

33. *El Comercio* 1997a, 2.

34. Furthermore, it would be the "youngest" member of the Executive Commission (the one who had served the least time on the commission) who would conduct the investigation, thereby guaranteeing that the task would fall to a provisional justice.

35. Clearly, the opposition foresaw this shortcoming with the slate of names they approved. Many observers believe that the opposition preferred to at least have the court up and running in order to protect individual rights. In its first case in November 1996, the Constitutional Court was asked to rule on the constitutionality of Law 26623 (which had extended the Executive Committee's oversight of the judicial branch until December 1998). The court found the law to be unconstitutional in a five-to-two ruling, but because the court did not reach the six-justice minimum, the law remained in effect. However, one article of Law 26623 was found to be unconstitutional in a separate six-to-one ruling. This article had allowed the Supreme Court chief justice to appoint another individual (Dellepiane) as the president of the Executive Commission. The court ruled that only the chief justice could be president of the commission. Thus, the Supreme Court chief justice (the vocal decano, Victor Castillo Castillo) became president of the Executive Commission. The chief justice then proceeded to name Dellepiane as the "executive secretary" of the Executive Commission and

transferred all the powers of the commission's president to its executive secretary.

36. For a detailed discussion of the Constitutional Court during this
period, see Conaghan 1998.

37. The court continued to hear cases of individual rights, which it may
do with a minimum quorum of four justices. The government continued to
give regular lip service to its intent to re-establish the Constitutional Court's
full membership, but the three seats remained vacant throughout the rest of
Fujimori's tenure.

38. Peru's electoral laws require a runoff election between the top two
candidates if no candidate receives a majority in the first round.

39. A third issue the judicial working group was to examine was Peru's
return to the jurisdiction of the OAS's Inter-American Court of Justice,
which the Fujimori administration had earlier refused to recognize.

40. The video showed an opposition congressman, Alberto Kouri, taking a $15,000 bribe in exchange for his support in Congress.

41. Fujimori also announced the deactivation of the National Intelligence Service, which had been overseen by Montesinos.

42. Law 27367 also deactivated the Executive Commission overseeing
the Public Ministry.

43. According to Peruvian law, the former president may not hold office
until the charges are cleared.

44. As to why he would leave the safety of Japan, speculation holds that
he believed he would be neither detained nor extradited (Chile had denied
Argentina's request to extradite former president Carlos Menem) and that
he saw Chile as a better location from which to conduct his re-election campaign (Paez 2005).

45. The World Bank, internal memo, n.d. In addition, USAID, after
having cut funding in 1992 in response to the *golpe*, reinstated funding for its
"one-stop" justice service centers in 1997 (USAID 2002, 90–91).

Chapter Four
Judicial Reform in Mexico in the 1990s

A version of this chapter was published as "Judicial Reform as Insurance
Policy: Mexico in the 1990s," *Latin American Politics and Society* 47: 1 (Spring
2005).

1. Cornelius and Craig describe a semiauthoritarian democracy as
characterized by competitive (though not necessarily fair and honest)

elections, which install governments more committed to political stability and labor discipline than to expanding democratic freedoms, protecting human rights, or mediating class conflicts (1991).

2. The PRI was built on *camarillas* (networks), with the president's network dominating the party during his term and dictating policy.

3. One of the most striking features of the 1917 constitution was the total absence of executive participation in the selection of the country's Supreme Court justices. The justices, who enjoyed life tenure, originally were nominated by state legislatures, voted on by secret ballot, and confirmed by an absolute majority in Congress. For detailed overviews of the Mexican judiciary in the twentieth century, see Fix-Zamudio 1988 and Fix-Zamudio and Cossío-Díaz 1996.

4. On average, each justice could appoint two judges per year. Particularly since 1980, when the federal judiciary began to expand and the number of judicial appointments per year increased dramatically, the selection of judges was marred by corruption and the importance of personal ties (Cossío-Díaz 1998a).

5. These included governorships, seats in the Senate and Chamber of Deputies, and positions with the federal executive.

6. However, a more favorable view of Mexican judicial independence is presented by Pablo González Casanova who states that out of the 3,700 Supreme Court cases between 1917 and 1960 in which the Mexican president was cited as the defendant, the court conceded protection to the plaintiff in one-third of its decisions. According to González Casanova, "One arrives at the conclusion that the Supreme Court works with certain independence with respect to the executive," but, he concedes, "that it, of course, follows the executive in important political areas and serves to provide it with stability" (1966, 36–37, author's translation).

7. Issues that have been excluded from *amparo* jurisdiction have included electoral matters, agrarian reform, the establishment of private schools, and the expulsion of foreigners (Fix-Fierro 1998, 4).

8. As before, constitutional provisions continue to prohibit decreasing judicial salaries while a judge holds office.

9. The Supreme Court still prepares its own budget, but the CFJ is responsible for the budget for the rest of the judicial branch.

10. Congress, however, is not bound to appropriate the amount requested by the CFJ.

11. For example, the court retains responsibility for compiling and publishing judicial decisions and the list of nominees from which the Chamber of Deputies names members to the Electoral Tribunal.

12. In Spanish, "unconstitutionality of laws" is written as *acciones de inconstitucionalidad* and is usually translated as "unconstitutionality of acts." I use the term *unconstitutionality of laws* because the Supreme Court may only use this power to invalidate laws passed by legislative bodies. This power of judicial review does not extend to executive decrees or other government acts or actions.

13. In 1996 the Mexican constitution was modified so that now political parties registered with the Federal Electoral Institute also have standing under the "unconstitutionality of laws" clause and enjoy the right to challenge electoral laws, even though they might not be represented in the legislature that passed the law.

14. The reform contains a major technical error. Under both of these constitutional control clauses, the case is not resolved if the agreement of eight justices is not achieved. According to Cossío-Díaz, this oversight was unintentional, and it needs to be rectified to allow court decisions that do not achieve supermajority agreement to take effect for the parties involved (1998b).

15. It is interesting that "electoral issues" were originally excluded from the purview of the Supreme Court's constitutional control clauses, an indication that the ruling party believed that it would not be able to control the postreform court as it had in the past.

16. Federal and state elections were scheduled for April 1997. The reform stated that those seeking to challenge an electoral law affecting these elections would have only fifteen days to petition the Supreme Court from the time the law was enacted and the court would have only fifteen days to respond. The reform's original thirty-day limit would be reinstated after that. In addition, the 1996 electoral reform placed the electoral tribunal, the body charged with resolving electoral disputes, under the judicial branch rather than under the executive, as it had been previously.

17. The 1996 electoral reform also granted standing to the directors of officially registered political parties to challenge electoral laws via the unconstitutional laws clause (in addition to a petition by one-third of the members of a legislature or the attorney general).

18. The opportunity to challenge existing laws, however, presents itself if the law is modified and replaced by the passage of a new law.

19. See Fix-Zamudio and Cossío-Díaz 1996 for detailed discussions of the Ley Reglamentaria and Ley Orgánica del Poder Judicial de la Federación (558–76).

20. For a detailed examination of the thirteen Supreme Court decisions addressing the constitutionality of electoral rules filed under the court's two new constitutional control clauses during Zedillo's *sexenio*, see Finkel 2003.

21. The invalidation of the governability clause in Quintana Roo applied only to that state, and governability clauses remained on the books of nearly half of Mexico's state legislatures at that time. Had the Supreme Court invalidated the federal electoral code, the ruling would have applied to all states, but because the court was ruling on a state law, the ruling did not affect the law in other states. Challenges to these clauses will have to wait until a new electoral code is passed in the particular state or until the national Congress addresses the issue in a modification of the federal electoral code. According to Corso (2000), the unanimous decision in the Quintana Roo case is a clear signal of way the court will rule on these cases in the future.

22. Opposition Congress members charged that Mexico's Union Bank had contributed millions of pesos to the PRI's campaign coffers in 1994 and, in exchange, had their private debt converted into public liabilities as part of a massive government bailout in 1995.

23. It should also be mentioned that the PRI was never a monolithic entity, and indeed, not all factions within the PRI were prepared to tolerate a real democratic opening in Mexico. PRI hardliners opposed relinquishing power, while "softliners" accepted the possible loss of PRI political control. Zedillo's network favored continuing with Mexico's democratic liberalization, even if it meant the loss of political power. As Zedillo and his network within the PRI accepted the potential loss of power, they had a real incentive to seek judicial empowerment and used their political power to carry it out.

24. However, the court's proposal did not provide for the unconstitutional laws clause; rather this clause came from the executive branch itself (Cossío-Díaz 1998b).

25. See http://web.worldbank.org/external/projects/.

26. For example, USAID's judicial funding for Mexico was targeted for establishing conferences between U.S. and Mexican judges, designing standards for judicial conduct, creating a pilot program to revamp the criminal justice system, and developing a speakers' program. See Perez 1998.

27. The only other party to have representation in Congress, also on the left side of the political spectrum, was the Workers' Party (PT). All eight of the PT's members voted in favor of the reform.

Bibliography

Abad Yupanqui, Samuel. 1995. "La Jurisdicción Constitucional en la Carta Peruana de 1993." In *Una Mirada a los Tribunales Constitucionales.* Lima: Comisión Andina de Juristas. 191–240.

Abad Yupanqui, Samuel, and Carolina Garcés Peralta. 1993. "El Gobierno de Fujimori Antes y Después del Golpe." In *Del Golpe del Estado a la Nueva Constitución*, edited by Abad Yupanqui and Garcés Peralta. Lima: Comisión Andino de Juristas. 85–190.

Acuna, Carlos, and Catalina Smulovitz, eds. 1995. *La Nueva Matrix Politica Argentina.* Buenos Aires: Ediciones Nueva Vision.

Aiyer, Sri-Ram. 1995. "Foreword." In *Judicial Reform in Latin America and the Caribbean: Proceedings of a World Bank Conference*, edited by Malcolm Rowat, Waleed H. Malik, and Maria Dakolias, vii. Washington, D.C.: The World Bank.

Ames, Barry. 1987. *Political Survival.* Berkeley: University of California Press.

Aranda, Jesus. 1999. "Objetan que el CJF Dependa de la Corte." *La Jornada* (March), http://www.jornada.unam.mx/1999/mar99/990323/repudian. html.

Bacque, Jorqe. 1995. "Corte Suprema de Justicia de la Nación: Cambio de Jurisprudencia en Materia de Derechos Individuales." *No Hay Derecho* no. 6: 12.

Baglini, Raúl, and Andrés D'Ambrosio. 1993. *Juicio a la Corte.* Buenos Aires: Baglini and D'Ambrosio.

Balzan, Mario. 1993a. "Menemistas y Radicales Siguen Negociando," *El Cronista*, September 20, p. 20.

———. 1993b. "El Gobierno Dice Que No Inducirá Cambios en la Corte Suprema." *El Cronista*, November 22, p. 22.

Barcesat, Eduardo. 1999. Constitutional Assembly representative. Personal interview with the author, Buenos Aires, March 17.

Basombrio, Carlos. 1997a. Director of the Institute for Legal Defense (*Instituto de Defensa Legal*). Personal interview with the author, Lima, July 3.

———. 1997b. Director of the Institute for Legal Defense (*Instituto de Defensa Legal*). Personal interview with the author, Lima, July 16.

Becker, G. S. 1968. "Crime and Punishment: An Economic Approach," *Journal of Political Economy* 76: 169–271.

Begné, Alberto. 1996. Political consultant. Personal interview with the author, Mexico City, July 14.

Bill-Chavez, Rebecca. 2003. "The Construction of the Rule of Law in Argentina: A Tale of Two Provinces," *Comparative Politics* 35:4 (July): 417–37.

———. 2004. *The Rule of Law in Nascent Democracies: Judicial Politics in Argentina*. Stanford: Stanford University Press.

Blum, Roberto E. 1997. "The Weight of the Past," *Journal of Democracy* 8:4 (October): 28–42.

Borea Odria, Alberto. 1996. "Un Tribunal en un Páramo de Autocracia." *Idéele* no. 88 (July): 11.

Boschi, Silvana. 1996. "El Proyecto Es un Engendro." *Clarín*, June 3, p. 6.

Buscaglia, Edgardo, Jr., Maria Dakolias, and William Ratliff. 1995. "Judicial Reform in Latin America: A Framework for National Development." Essays in Public Policy, no. 65, Hoover Institution, Palo Alto: Stanford University.

Calabresi, G. 1970 *The Costs of Accidents*. New Haven: Yale University Press.

Camp, Roderic Ai. 1993. *Politics in Mexico*. Oxford: Oxford University Press.

Cárdenas, Jaime. 1997. Mexican constitutional scholar and member of Mexico's Federal Electoral Institute. Personal interview with the author, Mexico City, April 23.

Caretas. 1993. "Carta Magna: El Cuerpo de Delito." July 1, p. 16.

———. 2000. "La Cofradia del Poder Judicial." November 2, p. 20.

Ciurlizza, Javier. 1999. "International Assistance and Judicial Reforms in Latin America." Andean Commission for Justice website, www.cajpe.org.pe/final.htm.

Clagett, Helen. 1952. *The Administration of Justice in Latin America*. New York: Oceana Publications.

Clarín. 1993a. "Piden Renuncias en la Corte Suprema." November 21, p. 5.

———. 1993b. "La UCR Admitió que Presiono para Lograr Cambios a la Corte." December 4, p. 5.

————. 1996a. "Fuerte Critica Judicial ante Menem por el Consejo de la Magistratura." May 29, pp. 2–3.

————. 1996b. "Polémica Jurídica." June 4, p. 2.

————. 1997a. "La Eleccion: Comicios Claves Que Trascienden la Renovacion Legislativa." October 26, internet edition.

————. 1997b. "La Eleccion: Es la Primera Vez Que Pierde el Peronismo Estando en el Poder." October 27, internet edition.

————. 1997c. "Informe Electoral." October 27, internet edition.

Coase, Ronald. 1937. "The Nature of the Firm." *Economica* 4 (November): 386–405.

————. 1960. "The Problem of Social Cost." *Journal of Law and Economics* 3: 1–44.

————. 1998. "The New Institutional Economics." *American Economic Review* 88: 2 (May): 72–74.

Comercio, El. 1992. "Confiep Denuncia Campana Orientada a Boicotear Reformas Estructurales." March 18, p. A4.

————. 1997a. "Magistrados Provisionales No Puede Tener Iqual Prerrogativa que Titulares." June 24, p. A2.

————. 1997b. "Se Iniciara Debate para Reforma Constitucional del Poder Judicial." August 3, A4.

————. 1997c. "La Reforma de la Administración de Justicia." August 6, p. A2.

————. 1998. "Polémico Futuro de la Reorganización en el Poder Judicial y la Fiscalia." November 23, p. A4.

Comisión Andino de Juristas. 1994. "Informe del Departamento de Estado de los EEUU al Congreso Sobre los Derechos Humanos en la Región Andina." *Boletín.* Lima: Comisión Andino de Juristas. 45–64.

Comisión de Juristas Internacionales. 1994. *Informe Sobre la Administración de Justicia en el Perú.* Lima: Comisión de Juristas Internacionales.

Conaghan, Catherine. 1998. "The Permanent Coup: Peru's Road to Presidential Reelection." *LASA Forum* 29:1 (Spring): 5–9.

Cornelius, Wayne A., and Ann L. Craig. 1991. *The Mexican Political System in Transition.* San Diego: Center for U.S.-Mexican Studies, University of California.

Corso, Edgar. 2000. Councilor to the chief justice of the Mexican Supreme Court. Personal interview with the author, Mexico City, June 19.

Cossío-Díaz, José Ramón. 1998a. Constitutional specialist. Personal interview with the author, Mexico City, August 27.

————. 1998b. Personal interview with the author, Mexico City, September 7.

Cubas, Victor. 1998. *La Cantuta: Cronica de la Investigacion Fiscal.* Lima: Palestra.

————. 1997a. Fiscal superior. Personal interview with the author, Lima, July 17.

————. 1997b. Fiscal superior. Personal interview with the author, Lima, July 24.

————. 2001. "Legal and Judicial Reform: The Role of Civil Society in the Reform Process." In *The Rule of Law in Latin America: The International Promotion of Judicial Reform,* edited by Pilar Domingo and Rachel Sieder. London: Institute of Latin American Studies, University of London.

Dalla Via, Alberto. 1999. Law professor, Universidad de Belgrano, Instituto de Investigaciones del Nuevo Estado. Personal interview with the author, Buenos Aires, March 2.

De Belaunde, Javier. 1991. "Aproximación a la Realidad de la Administración de Justicia en Perú." *Poder Judicial y Democracia.* Lima: Comisión Andino de Juristas.

De Soto, Hernando. 1986. *The Other Path: The Invisible Revolution in the Third World.* New York: Harper & Row.

Después de la Reforma de la Constitución. n.d. Biblioteca del Congreso de la Nacional, Buenos Aires, Argentina.

Diamond, Larry, Juan J. Linz, and Seymour Martin Lipset, eds. 1989. *Democracy in Developing Countries.* Vol. 4, *Latin America.* Boulder, Colo.: Lynne Rienner.

Dicey, A. V. 1939. *Introduction to the Study of Law and the Constitution.* 10th ed. London: Macmillan.

Dodson, Michael, and Donald Jackson. 2001. "Judicial Independence and Instability in Central America." In *Judicial Independence in the Age of Democracy,* edited by Peter Russell and David O'Brien. Charlottesville: University Press of Virginia. 251–72.

Domingo, Pilar. 1999. "Judicial Independence and Judicial Reform in Latin America." In *The Self Restraining State: Power and Accountability in New Democracies,* edited by Andrés Schedler, Larry Diamond, and Marc Plattner. Boulder, Colo.: Lynne Rienner.

————. 2000. "Judicial Independence: The Politics of the Supreme Court in Mexico," *Journal of Latin American Studies* 32:3 (October): 705–35.

Domingo, Pilar, and Rachel Sieder, eds. 2001. *The Rule of Law in Latin America: The International Promotion of Judicial Reform.* London: Institute of Latin American Studies, University of London.

Eguiguren, Francisco. 1997. Then head of the Judicial Academy. Personal interview with the author, Lima, July 9.

Estrada Samano, Rafael. 1995. "Administration of Justice in Mexico: What Does the Future Hold?" *United States–Mexico Law Journal* 3: 35–48.

European Commission for Democracy Through Law. 1994. *The Role of Constitutional Courts in the Consolidation of Democratic Governments.* Strasbourg: European Council Press.

Finkel, Jodi. 2003. "Supreme Court Decisions on Electoral Rules after Mexico's 1994 Judicial Reform: An Empowered Court." *Journal of Latin American Studies* 35: 777–99.

———. 2004. "Judicial Reform in Argentina in the 1990s: How Electoral Incentives Shape Institutional Change." *Latin American Research Review* 39: 3 (October): 56–80.

———. 2005. "Judicial Reform as Insurance Policy: Mexico in the 1990s." *Latin American Politics and Society* 47:1 (Spring): 87–113.

Fiss, Owen. 1993. "The Right Degree of Independence." In *Transition to Democracy in Latin America: The Role of the Judiciary,* edited by Irwin Stotzky. Boulder, Colo.: Westview Press.

Fix-Fierro, Hector. 1998. "Judicial Reform and the Supreme Court of Mexico: The Trajectory of Three Years." *US-Mexico Law Journal* 6 (Spring): 1–21.

Fix-Zamudio, Hector. 1988. "Setenta y Cinco Años del Evolucion del Poder Judicial en México." In *México Setenta y Cinco Años de Revolución,* edited by Otto Granados Roldán. Mexico City: Instituto Nacional de Estudios Históricos de la Revolución Mexicana. 289–382.

Fix-Zamudio, Hector, and José Ramón Cossío-Díaz. 1996. *El Poder Judicial en el Ordenamiento Mexicano.* Mexico City: Fondo de Cultura Economica.

Frühling, Hugo E. 1993. "Human Rights in Constitutional Order and in Political Practice in Latin America." In *Constitutionalism and Democracy: Transitions in the Contemporary World,* edited by Douglas Greenberg, Stanley N. Katz, Melanie Beth Oliviero, and Steven C. Wheatley. Oxford: Oxford University Press.

García Belaunde, Domingo. 1996. "La Reforma del Estado en Perú." In *La Reforma del Estado: Estudios Comparados,* edited by Jose Luis Soberanes, Diego Valades, and Hugo A. Concha. México City: UNAM.

———. 1997. Constitutional scholar and opposition member of Peru's 1992–93 constitutional convention. Personal interview with the author, Lima, July 23.

———. n.d. "La Reforma del Poder Judicial en el Perú." *Ius et Veritas.* Mimeo.

García-Lema, Alberto. 1994. *La Reforma por Dentro.* Buenos Aires: Planeta.

Geddes, Barbara. 1995. "A Comparative Perspective on the Leninist Legacy in Eastern Europe." *Comparative Political Studies* 28 (July): 239–74.

Ginsburg, Tom, 2000. "Does Law Matter for Economic Development? Evidence from East Asia." *Law and Society Review* 34:3: 829–56.

———. 2003. *Judicial Review in New Democracies: Constitutional Courts in Asian Cases.* Cambridge: Cambridge University Press.

González Casanova, Pablo. 1966. *La Democracia en México.* Mexico City: Editorial RA.

Grana, Eduardo. 1999. Judge and National Judicial Council member. Personal interview with the author, Buenos Aires, March 24.

Hammergren, Linn. 1998a. *The Politics of Justice and Justice Reform in Latin America.* Boulder, Colo.: Westview Press.

———. 1998b. "Promoting Rule-of-Law Reform: Lessons from Latin America." Carnegie Endowment for International Peace.

———. 1999. World Bank judicial sector specialist for Latin America. Personal interview with the author, Washington, D.C., September 7.

———. 2002a. "Fifteen Years of Judicial Reform in Latin America: Where Are We and Why Haven't We Made More Progress?" USAID Global Center for Democracy and Governance (March).

———. 2002b. "Do Judicial Councils Further Judicial Reforms? Lessons from Latin America." Working papers, Rule of Law series, Democracy and the Rule of Law Project, no. 28 (June). Carnegie Endowment for International Peace.

Harel, Rafael. 1998. Vice President of the Mexican Commission on the Defense and Promotion of Human Rights (Comisíon Mexicana por la defensa y la promocíon de los derechos humanos). Telephone interview with the author, Mexico City, September 29.

Hayes, Monte. 2005. "Fujimori Confident Courts Will Lift Arrest Orders, Allowing Him to Return to Peru." *Associated Press Worldstream,* October 6.

Helmke, Gretchen. 2002. "The Logic of Strategic Defection: Court-Executive Relations in Argentina Under Dictatorship and Democracy." *American Political Science Review* 96 (June): 291–303.

Herrera, Ricardo. 1998. Then head of the government's Judicial Coordinating Council. Personal interview with the author, Lima, November 23.

Hilbink, Elisabeth. 1999. "Legalism Against Democracy: The Political Role of the Judiciary in Chile, 1964–1994." Ph.D. diss., University of California–San Diego.

———. 2003. "An Exception to Chilean Exceptionalism: The Historical Roots of Chile's Judiciary and Prospects for Change." In *What Justice? Whose Justice? Fighting for Fairness in Latin America,* edited by Susan Eva Eckstein and Timothy Wickham-Crowley. Berkeley: University of California Press.

Hirschl, Ran. 2001. "The Political Origins of Judicial Empowerment Through Constitutionalization: Lessons from Israel's Constitutional Revolution." *Comparative Politics* 33:3 (April).

Iaryczower, Matias, Pablo Spiller, and Mariano Tommasi. 2002. "Judicial Independence in Unstable Environments, Argentina 1935–1998." *American Journal of Political Science* 46:4 (October): 699–716.

Instituto Nacional de Geografía e Informática. 1999. *Anuario de Estadísticos de los Estados Unidos Mexicanos 1998.* Aguascalientes: Instituto Nacional de Geografía e Información.

Inter-American Development Bank. 1993. "Report on the Reform of the Administration of Justice in Argentina." September 6.

———. 2006. "AR0124: Justice System Reform Support Program: Argentina." Inter-American Development Bank Projects, www.iadb.org.

Jarquín, Edmundo, and Fernando Carrillo, eds. 1998. *Justice Delayed: Judicial Reform in Latin America.* Washington, D.C.: Inter-American Development Bank; distr. Johns Hopkins University Press.

Jimenez, Juan. 1998. Legal expert, the Andean Commission of Jurists. Personal interview with the author, Lima, November 17.

Johnson, Kenneth. 1976. "Scholarly Images of Latin American Political Democracy," *Latin American Research Review* 11:2 (Spring): 129–39.

Joskow, Paul. 2004. "New Institutional Economics: A Report Card." Presidential address to the annual conference of the International Society of New Institutional Economics, Hungary, September 2003. http://econwww.mit.edu/faculty/download_pdf.php.

Kaplow, Louis, and Steven Shavell. 1999. "Economic Analysis of Law." In *Handbook of Public Economics,* vol. 3 (2002), edited by A. J. Auerbach and M. Feldstein.

Kelsen, Hans. 1945. *General Theory of Law and State.* New York: Russel and Russel.

Landes, William, and Richard Posner. 1975. "The Independence of Judiciaries in an Interest-Group Perspective." *Journal of Law and Economics* 18:3: 875–901.

Larkins, Christopher. 1996. "Judicial Independence and Democratization: A Theoretical and Conceptual Analysis." *American Journal of Comparative Law* 44:4 (Fall): 605–26.

———. 1998. "The Judiciary and Delegative Democracy in Argentina." *Comparative Politics* 30:4 (July): 423–42.

Latin American Regional Report—Southern Cone. 1997. "Menem Tries to Reassure His Troops." November 11, p. 6.

Latin American Research Review—Southern Cone. 1992. "Argentina Politics: Grip on Judiciary." October 15, p. 2.

Libecap, Gary. 1997. "The New Institutional Economics and Economic History." *Journal of Economic History* 57:3 (September): 718–21.

Lovatón Palacios, David. 2002. *Cambios en la Justicia Peruana y Sociedad Civil (1990–2002)*. Lima: Instituto de Defensa Legal.

Lovatón Palacios, David, and Wilfredo Ardito Vega. 2002. *Justicia de Paz: Nuevas Tendencias y Tareas Pendientes*. Lima: Instituto de Defensa Legal.

MacKay, Maria Luisa. 1993. "Cambiaria el Funcionamiento de la Corte como Parte del Acuerdo Político." *Clarín*, November 17, pp. 4–5.

Magaloni, Beatriz, and Arianna Sánchez. 2001. "Empowering Courts as Constitutional Veto Players: Presidential Delegation and the New Mexican Supreme Court." Paper presented at the American Political Science Association Conference, San Francisco, August 30–September 2.

Martínez, Victor. 1992. "Reforma Constitucional." *La Nación*, June 10, p. 9.

Matthews, R. C. O. 1986. "The Economics of Institutions and the Sources of Growth." *Economic Journal* 96:384 (December): 903–18.

Mauceri, Phillip. 1995. "State Reform, Coalitions, and the Neoliberal *Autogolpe* in Peru." *Latin American Research Review* 30:1: 7–37.

Melgar, Adalid, Mario. 1998. Federal Judicial Council Representative. Personal interview with the author, Mexico City, September 21.

Méndez, Juan. 1999. "Institutional Reform, Including Access to Justice: Introduction." In *The (Un)Rule of Law and the Underprivileged in Latin America*, edited by Juan Méndez, Guillermo O'Donnell, and Paulo Sergio Pinheiro. Notre Dame, Ind.: University of Notre Dame Press.

Merryman, John. 1985. *The Civil Law Tradition: An Introduction to the Legal Systems of Western Europe and Latin America.* Stanford: Stanford University Press.

Messick, Rick. 1999. "Judicial Reform and Economic Development: A Survey of the Issues." *The World Bank Observer* 14:1 (February): 117–36.

———. 2002. "Judicial Reform: The Why, the What, and the How." Paper presented at the conference Strategies for Modernizing the Judicial Sector in the Arab World, Marrakech, Morocco, March.

Molinelli, Guillermo. 1999. "La Corte Suprema de Justicia de la Nación Frente a los Poderes Políticos, a Traves del Control de Constitucionalidad, 1983–1998." Universidad de Buenos Aires. Mimeo.

Montoya Anguerry, Carlos. 1997. President of the National Magistrates Council 1995–98. Personal interview with the author, Lima, July 8.

———. 1998. President of the National Magistrates Council 1995–98. Personal interview with the author, Lima, November 16.

———. 2001. Legal scholar, La Catolica Law School, and president of the National Magistrates Council 1995–98. E-mail communication with the author, April 16.

Moody, John. 2000. Financial reporter, Bloomberg News. Personal interview with the author, Mexico City, June 18.

Morgan, Raúl. 1995. "La Corte Suprema, Antonio Lozano y Oscar Espinosa." *El Proceso* (Mexico City), September 11, 10:14.

Nación, La. 1983. "Quedo Constituida la Corte Suprema." December 3, p. 1.

———. 1988. "Elevarian a Nueve los Miembros de la Corte." January 4, p. 1.

———. 1990a. "Menem Abogo por un Régimen Presidencialista con Reelección." April 9, p. 3.

———. 1990b. "Males de la Justicia que Son Fuente de Injusticia." May 21, p. 1.

———. 1993a. "Peligra por la Corte el Acuerdo Reformista." November 22, p. 1.

———. 1993b. "El Gobierno Espera 'Gestos Patrióticos' en la Corte." November 23, p. 1.

———. 1995. "El Pliego de Vázquez, en Lista de Espera." December 1, p. 18.

———. 1996a. "Nazareno: No Hay Que Rifar la Corte." May 8, p. 8.

———. 1996b. "Menem Se Apuraría para Nombrar Jueces." May 30, p. 10.

———. 1997a. "Aeropuertos: Otro Si al Gobierno." International edition, December 16–22, p. 4.

————. 1997b. "La Alianza Analiza Pedir el Juicio Político." December 15–19, p. 8.

New York Times. 1992. "Peruvians Backing Leader's Actions." April 9, p. 2.

Nino, Carlos. 1993. "On the Exercise of Judicial Review in Argentina." In *Transitions to Democracy in Latin America: The Role of the Judiciary*, edited by Irwin Stotzky and Carlos Nino. Boulder: Colo.: Westview Press.

North, Douglass. 1990. *Institutions, Institutional Change, and Economic Performance.* Cambridge: Cambridge University Press.

North, Douglass, and Barry Weingast. 1989. "Constitutions and Commitment: The Evolution of Institutions Governing Public Choice in Seventeenth-Century England." *Journal of Economic History* 49:4 (December): 803–32.

Olson, Mancur. 1993. "Dictatorship, Democracy, and Development." *American Political Science Review* 87:3 (September): 567–76.

Oteiza, Eduardo. 1994. *La Corte Suprema: Entre la Justicia Sin Política y la Política Sin Justicia.* Buenos Aires: La Plata.

Paez, Angel. 2005. "Peru: Fujimori Carefully Orchestrated His Trip to Chile." *Inter Press Service*, November 8.

Pásara, Luis. 1998. "Judicial Reform and Civil Society." In *Justice Delayed: Judicial Reform in Latin America*, edited by Edmundo Jarquín and Fernando Carrillo. Washington, D.C.: Inter-American Development Bank; Baltimore, Md.: Distributed by Johns Hopkins University Press.

————. 2003. *Justicia y Sociedad Civil: El Papel de la Sociedad Civil in la Reforma Judicial, Estudios de Casos en Argentina, Chile, Colombia y Peru.* Santiago, Chile: Centro de Estudios de Justicia en las Americas.

Pellet Lastra, Arturo. 1999. Professor of law at the University of Buenos Aires. Personal interview with the author, Buenos Aires, February 5.

Penalosa, Pedro José. 1996. PRD legislative assistant, Mexico City Legislative Assembly. Personal interview with the author, Mexico City, July 22.

Perez, Patty. 1998. USAID legal consultant for Mexico. Personal interview with the author, Mexico City, September 11.

Popkin, Margaret. 2000. *Peace Without Justice: Obstacles to Building the Rule of Law in El Salvador.* University Park: Pennsylvania State University Press.

Portada (*La Republica*'s Sunday magazine). 1997. "Frustraciones de un Reformador." July 6, pp. 6–8.

Posner, Richard. 1970. *Economic Analysis and Law.* 1st ed. Boston: Little, Brown.

————. 1986. *Economic Analysis and Law.* Boston: Little, Brown.

Prillaman, William. 2000. *The Judiciary and Democratic Decay in Latin America*. Westport, Conn.: Praeger.

Quiroga Lavie, Humberto. 1999. Constitutional Assembly Representative. Personal interview with the author, Buenos Aires, March 24.

Rabossi, Eduardo. 1993. "Human Rights Violations in Argentina." In *Transitions to Democracy in Latin America: The Role of the Judiciary*, edited by Irwin Stotzky and Carlos Nino. Boulder, Colo.: Westview Press. 309–36.

Ramseyer, Mark. 1994. "The Puzzling (In)dependence of Courts: A Comparative Approach." *Journal of Legal Studies* 23 (June): 721–47.

Ramseyer, Mark, and Eric Rasmusen. 2003. *Measuring Judicial Independence*. Chicago: University of Chicago Press.

Republica, La. 1997. "Poder Judicial Debe Hacer su Propia Reforma." August 12, p. 1.

———. 1998. "Pezua Quiere un Ano Mas para la Reforma Judicial." November 11, p. 9.

Rodríguez Iturri, Roger. 1998. "Magistratura, Constitución y Libertad." *Idéele* no. 112 (October): 7.

Rodrik, Dani, Arvind Subramanian, and Francesco Trebbi. 2002. "Institutions Rule: The Primacy of Institutions over Geography and Integration in Economic Development." Centre for Economic Policy Research, NBER Working Paper 9305, National Bureau of Economic Research, Inc.

Rohter, Larry. 2000. "Surprise: Before He's Even Gone, Fujimori May Be Planning His Comeback." *New York Times*, September 21, p. A14.

Romero, Ismael. 1995. "Acuerda el PAN Fortalacer su Llamado Redimensionamiento." *La Jornada* (Mexico City), November 19, p. 12.

Rosenn, Keith S. 1987. "The Protection of Judicial Independence in Latin America." *University of Miami Inter-American Law Review* 19:1: 1–35.

Rospigliosi, Fernando. 1997. Political columnist. Personal interview with the author, Lima, July 15.

Rowat, Malcolm, Waleed H. Malik, and Maria Dakolias, eds. 1995. *Judicial Reform in Latin America and the Caribbean: Proceedings of a World Bank Conference*. Washington, D.C.: The World Bank.

Rubio, Marcel. 1998. Dean of La Católica University Law School. Personal interview with the author, Lima, December 1.

Russell, Peter. 2001. "Toward a General Theory of Judicial Independence." In *Judicial Independence in the the Age of Democracy*, edited by Peter Russell and David O'Brien. Charlottesville: University Press of Virginia. 1–24.

Saaba, Roberto. 1999. Law professor and head of the human rights watch group Citizen Power (*Poder Ciudadano*). Personal interview with the author, Buenos Aires, March 23.

Saez Garcia, Felipe. 1998. "The Nature of Judicial Reform in Latin America and Some Strategic Considerations." *American University International Law Review* 13:1267. Washington College of Law, American University.

Schedler, Andrés, Larry Diamond, and Marc Plattner, eds. 1999. *The Self Restraining State: Power and Accountability in New Democracies*. Boulder, Colo.: Lynne Rienner.

Schmidt, Gregory. 2000. "Delegative Democracy in Peru? Fujimori's 1995 Landslide and the Prospects for 2000." *Journal of Interamerican Studies and World Affairs* no. 1 (Spring): 99–132.

Serrano, Mónica. 1994. "The End of Hegemonic Rule? Political Parties and the Transformation of the Mexican Party System." In *Party Politics in "An Uncommon Democracy": Political Parties and Elections in Mexico*, edited by Neil Harvey and Mónica Serrano. London: Institute of Latin American Studies, University of London. 1–23.

Shapiro, Martin. 1981. *Courts: A Comparative and Political Analysis*. Chicago: University of Chicago Press.

Shihata, Ibrahim. 1995. "Judicial Reform and Developing Countries and the Role of the World Bank." In *Judicial Reform in Latin America and the Caribbean: Proceedings of a World Bank Conference,* edited by Malcolm Rowat, Waleed H. Malik, and Maria Dakolias. Washington, D.C.: The World Bank. 219–33.

Shirley, Mary. 2003. "What Does Institutional Economics Tell us About Development?" Paper presented at the International Society for New Institutional Economics annual conference, Budapest, Hungary, September.

Siedler, Rachel, ed. 1996. *Central America: Fragile Transition*. New York: St. Martin's Press.

Smulovitz, Catalina. 1995. "Constitucion y Poder Judicial en la Nueva Democracia Argentina: La Experiencia de las Instituciones." In *La Nueva Matrix Politica Argentina*, edited by Carlos Acuna. Buenos Aires: Ediciones Nueva Vision.

———. 1999. Political science professor at Universidad Torcuato di Tella. Personal interview with the author, Buenos Aires, March 24.

Solis, Dianne. 1994. "Weakened Giant: Calls for Reform Check Mexico's Mighty PRI as Elections Loom." *Wall Street Journal*, July 13, p. A1.

Statistical Abstract of Latin America. 2002. Edited by James Wilkie. Los Angeles: University of California Press.

Staton, Jeffrey. 2006. "Constitutional Review and the Selective Promotion of Case Results." *American Journal of Political Science* 50:1 (January): 98–112.

Stotzky, Irwin, ed. 1993. *Transition to Democracy in Latin America: The Role of the Judiciary.* Boulder, Colo.: Westview Press.

Stotzky, Irwin, and Carlos Nino. 1993. "The Difficulties of the Transition Process." In *Transition to Democracy in Latin America: The Role of the Judiciary,* edited by Irwin Stotzky and Carlos Nino. Boulder, Colo.: Westview Press.

Ugaz, Jose. 1997. Legal specialist. Personal interview with the author, Lima, July 11.

———. 2001. Special ad hoc prosecutor for the Peruvian government. Personal interview with the author, Los Angeles, January 11.

Unconstitutional Laws 6/98. Mexican Supreme Court, www.scjn.gobmx.

United States Agency for International Development. 2002. "Achievements in Building and Maintaining the Rule of Law." Occasional paper, November. Office of Democracy and Governance, www.usaid.gov.

Ventura, Adrián. 1995. "Amigos Son los Amigos." *La Nación,* December 3, p. 9.

———. 1998a. *El Consejo de la Magistratura.* Buenos Aires: Depalma.

———. 1998b. "Nazareno Decidio Convocar al Consejo de la Magistratura." *La Nación,* October 14, www.lanacion.com.ar/98/10/14/p10.htm.

———. 1999. Legal columnist for *La Nación.* Personal interview with the author, Buenos Aires, March 1.

Verbitsky, Horacio. 1993. *Hacer la Corte: La Construcion de un Poder Absoluto sin Justicia ni Control.* Buenos Aires: Planeta.

Verner, Joel. 1984. "The Independence of Supreme Courts in Latin America: A Review of the Literature." *Journal of Latin American Studies* 16: 463–506.

Waisman, Carlos. 1989. "Argentina: Autarkic Industrialization and Illegitimacy." In *Democracy in Developing Countries: Latin America,* edited by Larry Diamond, Juan J. Linz, and Seymour Martin Lipset. Boulder, Colo.: Lynne Rienner. 59–109.

Weldon, Jeffrey. 1997. "Political Sources of Presidencialismo in Mexico." In *Presidentialism and Democracy in Latin America,* edited by Scott Mainwaring and Matthew Shugart. Cambridge: Cambridge University Press.

Wiarda, H., and H. Kline, eds. 1985. *Latin American Politics and Economic Development.* Boulder, Colo.: Westview Press.

Williamson, Oliver. 2000. "The New Institutional Economics: Taking Stock, Looking Ahead." *Journal of Economic Literature* 38:3 (September): 595–613.

Workshop on Law and Economic Development. 2005. "Introduction." *International Review of Law and Economics* 25: 62–64.

World Bank. 1991. *World Development Report.* Washington, D.C.: The World Bank.

———. n.d. "Selected World Bank and IDB Judicial and/or Legal Reform Projects." Internal bank memo, on file with author.

Xinhua News Agency. 2004. "Fujimori Delivers Paper to Peruvian Court to Defend Himself." March 25, http://web.lexis-nexis.com/universe/printdoc.

Zamorano, Carlos. 1999. Co-president of the Argentine League for the Rights of Man (Liga Argentina por los derechos humanos). Personal interview with the author, Buenos Aires, March 11.

Zedillo, Ernesto. 1995. State of the Union Address. *Informe Presidencial.* Mexico City, September 6.

Index

Jodi S. Finkel

is associate professor of political science

at Loyola Marymount University.